You Can Still Make It
In The Market

Nicolas Darvas

You Can Still Make It In The Market

NICOLAS DARVAS

author of How I Made $2,000,000 In The Stock Market

"When developing my representation of stock behavior I had always had at the back of my mind the idea that it would finally take the form of a simple portable device to be carried around in the pocket, to be checked against each day's closing prices. It would be no bigger than a postcard but yet would contain its own built-in instructions and all the information necessary to make investment decisions, based on my theories, on whether to BUY, SELL, or HOLD. It would, in short, be a compact visual representation of my system. This gave me the clue I needed, I decided to call it ... DAR-CARD."

PART I

Dar•Card°

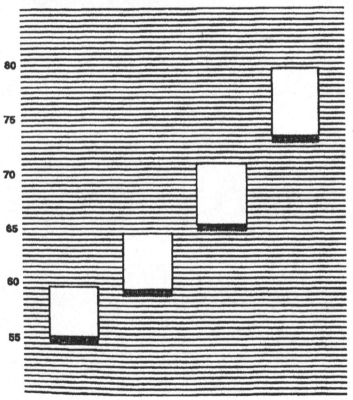

Chapter One

In the fall of 1974, while on a business trip to London, I received a most unusual request. I was invited to address an investment seminar to be attended by a distinguished gathering of British stock-market experts, brokers, and investment managers.

I was very surprised to receive this request since it was just these members of the stock-market establishment who had in the past always scoffed at my investment theories and achievements. Although my methods had been highly successful and had proved themselves over and over again they were generally regarded by such professionals as extremely unorthodox and even heretical. So I would not have thought that they would be the slightest bit interested in hearing my highly personal views on the stock market. I was assured, however, that my books and opinions, though controversial, were well known in Britain and that my appearance would be the highlight of the seminar and would give British investors their first opportunity of meeting and questioning me. I therefore gladly accepted the invitation.

I gave a lot of thought to how I could best present my views to what I anticipated would be a somewhat antagonistic audience intent on shooting me down. My problem was how to present my highly unconventional approach to the market, and particularly my "Box Theory," in a clear and simple form. It had to be both convincing and immediately understandable even to the most unsophisticated investor. My investment technique had always been largely a mental one; as a result of long experience and observation, stock-market movements were always firmly established in my mind. I never looked at charts and paid no attention to the balance sheets and similar "fundamentals" when deciding on my actions. But how could I convey such a maverick's method in the most effective way?

My theatrical instinct (I had been a stage and nightclub dancer for many years before I became interested in the stock market) made me aware of the need for visual impact and dramatic presentation which would grip and hold my audience, many of whom would be hearing about my theories and techniques and the reasoning behind them for the first time. I needed something more powerful than a mere chart. I required a method of graphically representing the behavior of stocks which would show at a glance the trend, the buying and selling points, and indicate *automatically* what action to take at every stage. It had to be, in short, nothing less than the philosopher's stone of the stock market—it would convert data directly into action and profits.

Necessity is the mother of invention, it has been truly said. My acceptance of the seminar invitation forced on me the need to solve this problem quickly. Strolling through Hyde Park in London in the weeks before the seminar I constantly cast my mind back to the successful stocks that had made so much money for me in my early days in the market—Lorillard, Thiokol, Fairchild Camera —and those with which I have been equally successful more recently—Tandy, Centronic Data, and Digital Equipment—to mention just a few. What had they all got in common, I asked myself? Why had I taken the action I did? What led me to my decisions? And above all— how could I explain and illustrate my mental processes to an outsider?

For weeks I turned these questions over and over in my mind, searching for an answer and trying out various possible solutions. I relived all my past successes and failures in an attempt to extract the essential lessons they had taught me about stock-market investment and represent them in graphic form. Slowly but surely a picture began to form and develop in my mind. Then one day—Eureka! I stumbled on exactly what I was looking for. It was so simple I wondered why it had taken me so long to see it. It showed everything one needed to know in a nutshell and provided a clearer insight into the action of stocks than anything I had previously seen. It was just what I needed.

In the days preceding the seminar I continued to concentrate on my new discovery, turning its possibilities over in my mind. The more I pondered it the greater its potential seemed to become. Having discovered the basic idea it seemed only natural to try to extend and develop it. It had started out as merely a method of illustrating the behavior of stocks, but could it, I asked myself, be converted into an all-embracing investment tool that provided the answer to any stock-market problem that might arise? How wonderful it would be, I thought, if I could create for every stock a simple compact diagram—no bigger than a postcard—that would show everything necessary for investment decisions. Could I even incorporate into it my other indispensable investment tool—the stop-loss? In view of the complexity of the problem and the infinite variety of stock-market situations it seemed at first sight a daunting and almost insuperable task. But its potential seemed so immense that I began to think in terms of something much more universal than the simple pictorial seminar representation I had originally evolved.

Eventually, after much trial and error and many wastepaper baskets full of rejected attempts I finally drew what seemed to me the simplest and clearest representation of my successful method. I admired it for days—like an art collector who has just acquired a new Rembrandt. I was proud of the results of my efforts and elated that I had at last licked the problem. But when the first flush of excitement and enthusiasm had worn off I had to admit that I was somewhat disappointed. I was searching for the philosopher's stone, for a new key to stock-market profits, and all I had come up with was a rather primitive diagram. It was true that it contained all the information necessary to make immediate investment decisions but I had to confess that its appearance would never set the world on fire. It was scientifically and factually right but artistically and esthetically wrong. No one, I felt sure, would be moved to take any action on the basis of this uninspiring diagram.

I put the problem to a graphic designer who had worked for me in the past. I explained to him what I was trying to achieve and the reasoning behind it. "It contains all the necessay data, but there is something wrong with it," I said.

He diagnosed the trouble immediately. "As it stands, it has no drama. The boxes don't look like boxes and the stop-loss makes them look even more unreal and unbalanced. Whatever investment merits it may have, visually it's dull and uninteresting and no one would give it a second glance in its present form." I might be a stock-market expert but I was obviously no Rembrandt!

He took away my crude primitive drawing and agreed

to modify it and add what he felt were the missing in-
gredients without altering the basic concept. I was curious to see what would emerge.

He rang me up a few days later. "I think I've got what
you want," he said. "I'll bring it round right away." I was
astonished to see what he had achieved. My dull uninteresting boxes were now truly three-dimensional, their
relationship to each other clearly and sharply outlined.
The stop-loss area, far from appearing like an artificial
appendage, now looked more like an indication of a
danger area for each box—not just a line but an *area*
which shouted a warning: "DANGER! If your stock
enters this area, watch out, you are in trouble." Also the
prices, which I had originally put on the boxes themselves, had been removed to a scale at the side, giving
the boxes a clear, uncluttered look which enhanced their
effect. The result was stunning, and I could see immediately that I now had a unique and unrivaled investment
tool.

All it needed now was a name. It was not a chart, it
was not a graph. It was not, strictly speaking, even a
price history of the stock. It was more than a passive
representative of historic price behavior. I toyed with
names like Boxgram, Stock Action, Share Indicator,
etc., but these did not appeal to me—they were much
too dull and technical.

When developing my representation of stock behavior I had always had at the back of my mind the

idea that it would finally take the form of a simple portable device to be carried around in the pocket, to be checked against each day's closing prices. It would be no bigger than a postcard but yet would contain its own built-in instructions and all the information necessary to make a decision, based on my theories, on whether to BUY, SELL, or HOLD. It would, in short, be a compact visual representation of my system. This gave me the clue I needed, I decided to call it . . .

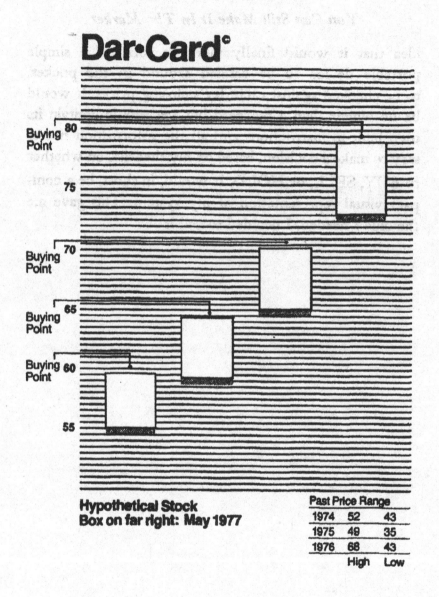

Dar•Card©

Buying Point — 80

75

Buying Point — 70

Buying Point — 65

Buying Point — 60

55

Hypothetical Stock
Box on far right: May 1977

Past Price Range		
1974	52	43
1975	49	35
1976	68	43
	High	Low

HOW I DRAW A DAR-CARD

A. When the price of a rapidly rising stock reaches a resistance point which it does not surpass for three or more consecutive days, that point represents the top of the box.

B. If, after falling from the upper limit, the stock reaches a downward resistance point which it does not penetrate for three or more consecutive days, that level represents the bottom of the box.

C. The shaded danger level is indicated when the price falls 5 percent below the bottom of the box.

HOW I USE THE DAR-CARD

A. A stock is in a rising trend when it is in its topmost box. As long as it remains there its price fluctuations should be ignored and the stock is a HOLD.

B. If the price of the stock moves above the top of this topmost box the stock becomes a BUY. A 10 percent stop-loss should be set on the first breakout.

C. Having formed a new higher box, if the price falls below the bottom into the shaded area of this box the stock is a SELL.

D. There is no reason to HOLD or BUY a stock that is not in its topmost box.

The DAR-CARD seemed to me to be such a remarkably clear-cut and unambiguous indicator, completely unlike the hit-and-miss methods generally employed, that I had no doubt that it would be greeted with enthusiasm by my audience. Having finalized it in the form I wanted, all I needed to do now was to demonstrate its effectiveness in practical investment situations and show how easily it provided the answer to many perennial stock-market problems.

I knew from my own correspondence that there is no end to the problems and questions different types of investors have. Since my first books were written I have been constantly bombarded with questions about the stock market and my investment methods, and with requests for my opinions on an enormous variety of investment matters. These questions have come from both new and experienced investors, from the proverbial "widows and orphans" and from hardened professionals. The questions have covered all aspects of the stock market from the most elementary to the most sophisticated: "How do I find growth stocks?"; "Should I buy blue chips?"; "Should I buy stocks for dividends or capital gains?"; "What makes a growth stock?"; "When is the best time to buy and sell?"; and of course the perennial plea, "Do you know a good stock?"

The fact that such questions are still being asked gradually made me realize how little the stock market is understood by the majority of investors, and how few really know how to handle stocks successfully. Despite the enormous amount of advice, tips, and analysis churned out day after day by the financial press the fact is that many investors are completely confused and bemused by the stock market, its behavior and workings, and are largely unaware of the factors that determine stock prices. Many investors seem to have little idea what to do under different circumstances, how to make big profits, and how to avoid big losses.

I can hardly blame them. When I first became involved with the stock market I was in much the same position. When I bought my first shares of stock some twenty years ago I had no idea that in reality I was a Daniel buying a ticket of admission to the lion's den. But that is exactly what I was doing—I was an innocent and ignorant amateur offering himself for sacrifice to the maw of the market. I knew absolutely nothing about the stock market. I did not even know that there was one in New York or that stockbrokers earned their living from the commission they made on my buying and selling—commission that came off my profits, incidentally. I bought stock in companies whose names I could not pronounce; what they did or what they made I had no idea. There could have been no more clueless, unsophisticated operator than I was.

My major problem was how to learn about the stock market and how to operate in it successfully. Unfortunately, I found most of the experts and books on the subject virtually useless. All I got from them was mumbo-jumbo about earnings, dividends, asset values, price-earnings ratios, etc., until my head was spinning. They seemed to be able to tell me everything except what I wanted to know, and that was simply: how do I make money in the market? None of the methods they recommended seemed to work despite the claims made for them. It was this that led me to go my own way, find out for myself by trial and error, and develop my own successful method.

This therefore seemed to be a wonderful opportunity of answering the many questions that had been fired at me over the years. Indeed, using the DAR-CARD I could now give clearer and more easily understood answers than I could have done previously. I was not, however, interested in purely academic questions; I wanted to answer the questions of the ordinary investors, big and small, many of whom do not know where to turn for solutions. What better way to do this than by actually asking people what their stock-market problems were? I meet different kinds of people from all walks of life every day. By simply asking them I was bound to obtain an enormous variety of practical investment problems. And they would be *real* problems based on everyday happenings, the sort of situations that often make investors tear their hair in frustration.

So whenever I got into conversation with anyone I would ask them about their stock-market experiences and problems. I was truly amazed at some of the things I was told. The ignorance and naiveté of some investors astonished me—like the company president of a multi-million-dollar company who still believed that the price of a company's stock was directly related to its earnings, when a glance at any stock tables would have shown him that a company's earnings can go up while its stock price goes down, and vice versa. Or the many innocent investors who still buy stock for dividend income when a simple calculation would show them that the return they receive by way of dividends is less than they would get by simply keeping their money on deposit in a bank —and at less risk! Or the countless investors who average down in a bear market until they have lost almost their entire capital when they should have cleared out of the market with their money intact when the slide first started. It was almost incredible the mistakes that people made and the sheer bad advice they were given.

So the invitation to the seminar had two quite un-expected consequences—it led me to develop the DAR-CARD and it made me aware of the need for a book which would not only answer investors' questions in a clear and simple way but would also restate some of the basic truths about stocks which many people appear to have lost sight of. I decided that the best way to do this would be to describe my recent experiences in today's stock market, the actions I took, and the reasons behind them.

Chapter Two

It was the closing months of 1974 and the stock market had been in a steep decline for nearly two years—one of the worst bear markets in living memory. No stock had been left untouched by the slaughter and many were selling at less than three times earnings. Practically every stock, from the mightiest to the lowliest, had been savaged, and there was gloom and despondency everywhere. People were talking as if the market was finished, dead and buried; it was 1929 all over again.

I could hardly have evolved the DAR-CARD at a worse time—there was just no opportunity to use it or to demonstrate its value. I felt like a general who discovers a master plan for victory only to find that the war is over. I had no choice but to sit patiently and wait for the right opportunity to arrive.

Over the years I had developed the habit of constantly watching the market for promising new stocks in future growth industries. I was not interested in "widows and orphans" stocks, in institutional favorites, like IBM, General Motors, or U.S. Steel. These companies were now so enormous and had so many shares outstanding that it would require literally a stampede by investors to make their shares double in price. I watched for the IBMs and General Motorses of the future—the blue chips of to-morrow, not the blue chips of today or yesterday. I was looking for stocks that would triple and quadruple in the next bull market, not those that would have to struggle to make ten points.

This approach had always paid off in the past. I had found such champion stocks not by reading the financial columns of the newspapers, or subscribing to advisory services, or even by asking my broker. I had simply watched the market quotations until they popped up in front of my eyes, impelled upwards by the forces of supply and demand. No company with a promising future goes unnoticed in the market—there are too many knowl-edgeable and hawk-eyed professionals around for that. I would simply wait, watch, and see what stocks were going up on high volume.

Experience and practice had trained my eyes to notice such stocks in the early stages of their rise, to separate them from the others by their technical action, and to spot them in the confusing noisy background of market fluctuations in which they lay buried. If they were there I knew from my past success that I would be able to discover them very quickly. It would then be merely a question of getting into them as soon as possible with as much capital as I could muster. But at the same time I would act with the caution of a battle-scarred veteran of many stock-market battles, not with the reckless over-confidence of a green rookie. I knew that I could be wrong in my reading of the market and I was always ready to run if things didn't go as I expected.

One thing I knew for certain—I would have to find new stocks, not the ones I had held years ago. Those sprightly young Olympic athletes of stocks that I had bought in previous bull markets, that had sprinted ahead of the field making a fortune for me in the process, were now decrepit old men with one foot in the grave. The companies they represented had reached and passed their prime; they were now respected, conservative senior citizens, and their stock behaved likewise. They had earned their place in stock-market history and I would always look back on them with nostalgia and happy re-membrance of exciting times spent together. But like any champion horse that has had its day the time had come to put them out to graze and turn my attention to to-morrow's young runners.

So I carefully watched the quotations for any signs of life in what to most people seemed a lifeless corpse. I knew the market would not go on falling forever. When all the sellers had left to lick their wounds swearing "Never again," when all the stock-market doc-tors had pronounced the patient dead before the ink was even dry on the death certificate the market would sud-denly and unexpectedly come to life. It would surprise everyone with its new-found agility, as if someone had sneaked in when no one was looking and given it a sip of the elixir of life.

To my delight, I was not wrong. Looking at the stock tables in September–October 1974 my instinct told me that the market was coming to life. It was no more than a flickering of the eyelids, so to speak, but there was no mistaking it. Towards the end of September I suddenly noticed that Hughes Tool had jumped more than ten points in one week on enormously increased volume. By the middle of November the price of the stock had doubled from a low of 36¾ to a high of 72¼. Moreover, all around me stocks were rapidly coming to life. The market was on the move—I could feel it!

Then like a tidal wave appearing without warning all stocks big and small were swept up in a colossal surge as the forces of the market were suddenly released. I should have felt elated—after all I had a brand new weapon for just this situation. But I was petrified! The behavior of the market was like nothing I had ever seen before. Could my eyes be deceiving me? Was I so anxious to try out the DAR-CARD that my eyes were tricking me into believing that the bear market was over? Was I indulging in mere wishful thinking? Perhaps it was just another false breakout which I in my impatience was interpreting as the beginning of a new bull market. Reason and emotion fought together inside me as I tried to make up my mind. I could see other stocks roaring away in front of my eyes—Houston Oil leaping from 12 to 26 in a mere three weeks in October—and I sat hypnotized like a frightened rabbit, afraid to act.

The fact of the matter was that the long period of inactivity since the last bull market and the long wait during the devastating bear market had taken its toll of my emotions. I was stale and scared. My stop-loss had taken me out of stocks early in 1973, and apart from one or two perfunctory sorties into the market I had hardly touched a stock for two years. So although I had been on the alert, ready for the revival, I had been caught flat-footed and muscle-bound when it happened.

Chapter Three

There was one thing I found most disconcerting. No stocks seemed to be forming boxes. Hughes Tool and Houston Oil, for example, had gone up in a dead straight line without as much as a pause for breath. Many other stocks behaved in exactly the same way. The upswing of the market was so sharp and widespread that I found it virtually impossible to distinguish the truly strong stocks from the weaker ones. Was my method finished, fit only to be thrown on to the rubbish heap of stock-market history? Or was the market simply going through a temporary, once-for-all phase of readjustment after the long depressing bear market in which countless stocks had lost up to 80 percent of their value?

As if to restore my faith and confidence I reviewed the situation over and over again. I was convinced I must stick to my method and principles. I had forged and tested my techniques many times in the hot furnace of the market. They had proved themselves time and time again, and if I departed from them the result could only be disaster. On the other hand I knew I must not allow my method to become a straitjacket. Perhaps the market had changed its character permanently. To adhere blindly and rigidly to my approach whatever happened could be fatal. Consistency, as Oscar Wilde once said, is the characteristic of weak minds. I must leave room for some flexibility; it might, after all, become necessary to make some modifications to my approach.

Until the picture became clearer I must resist at all costs the temptation to be merely "in the market." I was looking for the right stock that would give me big capital gains. As in the past, I could see no point in wasting my time and money on, for example, supermarket and textile stocks. The most such companies could hope for would be to push up sales by 10 percent—if they were lucky. No! I would keep my eyes on those industries that had an interest in things to come—electronics, space science, semiconductors, lasers. Something new and exciting would eventually come up, I was certain.

I also reminded myself that there were many stocks that I must not touch under any circumstances. Much as I liked them, whenever I had bought them in the past they had done me an injury. We were completely incompatible temperamentally. They were like beautiful women whom I must only admire from afar but with whom I knew I must never have an affair because they would cause me nothing but trouble. They were not for me.

So for the time being, I told myself, I will wait for my opportunity to arrive and let the market tell me what to do.

At the beginning of February 1975, after nearly two months of nail-biting, frustrating inactivity, my patience was rewarded. I noticed a sudden jump of three and a half points on the week in National Semiconductor—an old friend of mine with which I was familiar. The price rise alone was perhaps not very spectacular, but what especially attracted my attention was a huge rise in volume, from a normal weekly turnover of around one hundred thousand shares in December and January to about seven hundred thousand in the first week of February. There was obviously an enormous interest awakening in this stock, an interest I could hardly ignore.

In addition, to my great joy, I could see the stock price forming boxes right there in front of me. The share price had been almost stagnant for weeks, varying in a narrow 9–11 box. It had now broken out on high volume into a 14–17 box. I was jubilant—my theory still worked after all! As though rewarding me for my patience and faith and for my refusal to be panicked by the rising market, National Semiconductor seemed to be beckoning me to come aboard in time for takeoff.

The technical action was right. The industry was right (the company was a leader in the new and expanding field). It seemed to be just the stock I had been waiting for.

Dar•Card©

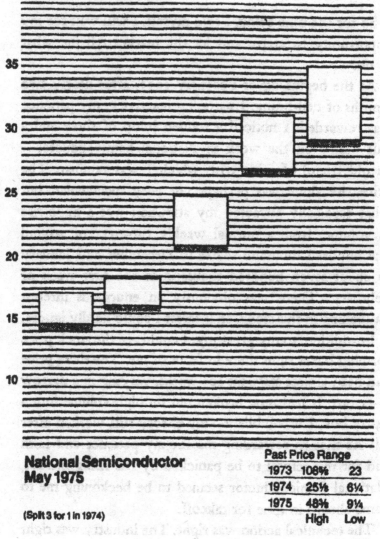

35

30

25

20

15

10

**National Semiconductor
May 1975**

(Split 3 for 1 in 1974)

Past Price Range		
1973	106⅜	23
1974	25½	6¼
1975	48⅜	9¼
	High	Low

24

By the time I first became interested in National Semiconductor it had already practically doubled in price in a mere two months and to many people it might have seemed as though I had missed the boat. I could have bought it at 8½ in December, but the price of a stock alone is never a sufficient basis for buying it. Sure, National Semiconductor was cheap at 8½ and if I had bought it then I would have been sitting pretty.

But experience long ago taught me to beware of bargains. Before I would touch any stock I first wanted to see some evidence that it was going to go up and get dearer. Of course, using this approach I would never be able to boast that I had bought at the bottom, but that didn't worry me. I was trying to make big profits while reducing the margin of error to a minimum; I was not interested in trying to impress my broker with how clever I was to have bought at the bottom. The stock market is no place for vanity. I did not care if I lost the first few points of a big rise. Those few points were just an insurance premium that I willingly paid to ensure that I was not buying a completely dud stock. I always thought of the well-known Wall Street maxim "Buy cheap and sell dear" as just another cliché that I have long since dumped in the dustbin. It is a far better policy, I have found, to buy "dear" and sell "dearer."

One factor, however, did give me reason to pause. I would normally not buy a stock unless, in addition to satisfying the requirements of my Box Theory, it had also broken through its all-time high. This was merely an additional safety requirement—when a stock has not only reached a new high but has also surpassed its all-time high it can safely be assumed that all those hapless people who had bought it at the top and had been waiting for an opportunity to get out would have sold out by now. They would thus no longer be a drag on the stock and the price would surge forward. National Semiconductor, however, was nowhere near its all-time high. My problem was—should I wait for the all-time high to be breached, just to be on the safe side, or buy it now as soon as it showed signs of breaking out of its present box?

It was an agonizing dilemma. Stocks had fallen so far in the past two years that if I waited for the price to reach the all-time high I could be waiting till kingdom come. The bull market might even be all over before I had put a single cent into any stock!

I had to make a quick now-or-never decision. I decided to forget all about the all-time high. The bear market had been so severe and stocks had fallen so far and so fast, I reasoned, that it could safely be assumed that all weak holders of the stock would have abandoned it by now. To wait for the all-time high under such circumstances would be carrying caution to ridiculous extremes. In any case if I was wrong my safety net, the stop-loss, would be there as ever to ensure that I suffered no injury. The opportunity was too good to miss.

I immediately rang my broker and instructed him to buy 5,000 shares at 17½ with a stop-loss at 14½. Although I tried hard to adopt a cool, calm demeanor my hands were shaking as I gave him the order. The market had been roaring up for two months now and I had been left behind on the sidelines, a mere helpless spectator. Try as I might I just could not keep my emotions suppressed. I felt scared and apprehensive. When I put the receiver down I felt as if I had just placed a bet. I was betting on the validity of my theory, betting that the market still obeyed the same rules and that my reading of it was correct. There was now nothing I could do but watch to see how my stock would perform.

In the days which followed National Semiconductor behaved in a maddeningly indecisive manner. It moved up into a 16¼–18⅜ box and seemed to stay there interminably without making any decisive breakout. I was disappointed but had no choice but to hold on and wait. At last at the beginning of March the strong breakout I was waiting for came. National Semiconductor jumped over 20 and made a new 21–24 box. I was elated; it was just like old times. I was back in action again and things were now going my way. The next decision I would have to make would be when the time had come to ride with the trend and buy some more.

As the stock started to move decisively ahead and rose to 27 I gave my broker instructions to buy another 5,000 shares with a stop-loss for my total holdings at 26. Although the price was well above my original purchase price I still took steps to protect myself against any unexpected reversal. I did not want to lose the profit I had already made.

But National Semiconductor continued to behave beautifully. By the middle of April it had risen over 35 and I had already doubled my original investment. I was walking on air, I smiled at everyone, I had not felt so good-humored and happy for months. What a wonderful effect a rising stock can have on your spirits! I was in the market again and winning. Gone was the uncertainty, the soul searching, the frustration I had felt a mere three months before. I was master of the situation once again and I revelled in it.

But I had forgotten one thing. Stocks don't like to be taken for granted. In some perverse way they have a habit of springing surprises and delivering a hearty slap in the face to anyone who is arrogant enough to think he has mastered them. While I was still feeling on top of the world National Semiconductor unexpectedly went into reverse. After hesitating between 33 and 35 and dropping momentarily to 31 the stock suddenly fell below 30.

My warm optimism rapidly evaporated and was replaced by the cold chill of fear. I hurriedly phoned my broker and raised my stop-loss to 29⅝. No sooner had I done so than I was sold out! I hardly knew what hit me. One minute I was in the market happily holding a rising stock, and the next minute I was out in the cold again. My honeymoon with National Semiconductor had lasted a mere three months. Although I had made a useful profit I felt acute disappointment and chagrin. I had hardly had a chance to get my toes wet in the market before I was kicked out and left high and dry.

But the stock was not finished with me yet. After dropping to 28 it turned its nose up at me, turned round quickly and within a week had risen above 35 once more. I had been sold out on a false move!

I felt mortified; I was filled with the urge to rush in and buy it back again. But since there was no way of knowing how long the run would last I had no choice but to wait until it leveled off and formed a new box.

This eventually happened. The stock rose to a new 35–38 box. I rang my broker and gave instructions to buy back my stock if it rose above 38, with a stop-loss at 35. Within a few days I received confirmation that my buy order had been executed.

The boxes continued to pile up and in June the price

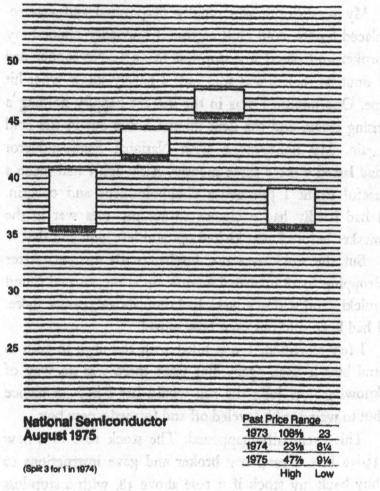

Dar·Card©

50

45

40

35

30

25

National Semiconductor
August 1975

(Split 3 for 1 in 1974)

Past Price Range		
1973	108⅝	23
1974	23⅛	6¼
1975	47⅞	9¼
	High	Low

pushed over 40. Although the slap in the face I had received from the stock's rapid turnaround had given me a more sober attitude towards it, it was difficult to suppress the excitement I felt as it pushed relentlessly higher and higher—42–45–47.

There seemed to be no holding it back but I was taking no chances now. I continued to move my stop-loss up as the stock rose, ready to sell out at a moment's notice if the price dropped below the bottom of its box. In July the stock rose to a high of 47⅞, hesitated, dropped, and rose again but without much conviction. I sensed trouble, I reached for the telephone and quickly raised my stop-loss to 43. Within two days I was sold out. Once again National Semiconductor and I had parted company.

Chapter Five

I have often wondered why so many people just as experienced and knowledgeable in stock-market matters as myself make such a mess of their stock-market trading. Everything they do seems to go wrong. They buy at the top and sell at the bottom, take small profits and sit on large losses, and generally do the opposite of what common sense suggests they should do. My handling of National Semiconductor did not involve any special skills, abstruse calculations, or inspired guesses. The behavior of the stock itself told me what to do—when to buy, when to play safe, and when to sell out. I merely had to protect myself at *every stage* against any unexpected happening by using the stop-loss. Why is it that so many people find stocks so difficult to cope with successfully?

There is no human activity that I know of to which people have a more irrational approach than the stock market. There seems to be something hypnotic about stocks that makes people behave in a manner which they would never do in any other field of activity. People's irrationality in the stock market often takes the most bizarre forms. Two anecdotes will serve to illustrate some of the curious mental blockages from which many suffer when they are involved with stocks.

I am very friendly with a successful investor in Las Vegas whom I often visit for social reasons and for discussions about the stock market. I do this not because we need each other's advice but because talking to him is like recharging my mental batteries. He has a market flair that is truly amazing. He can predict with almost consistent correctness how the market will behave in the coming months. He does this purely by a unique feeling for the market that he has developed over many years of studying its behavior.

Having made a tidy sum in stocks he decided to sell his services to the public by starting a market advisory service. He proposed to send out to subscribers a fortnightly market letter giving his predictions on the future course of the market. It seemed a good idea and when I left him for a trip to Europe he was getting all ready to set up in business.

On my return eighteen months later I made a point of looking him up. I was somewhat mystified to find that his venture had been a complete flop. Although his predictions and readings of the market had been remarkably accurate and he had predicted the coming bear market and advised his readers to sell, he had lost 70 percent of his subscribers in the months that followed and had to close down the business.

Why? Because to be successful an advisory service must tell people what they *want to hear*, not necessarily what the truth is. When the market is soaring people want to be told what to buy and to be reassured that the trend will continue; they do not want to be told to be prepared to get out because a major reversal is imminent. They constantly want to be given optimistic reports and tips which will enable them to make money. They do not want to be told to sell out or stay out of the market even though it may be in their best interests to do so. My friend's analyses were correct but he was out of tune with the *emotions* of his readers. They regarded his opinions as nonsensical and therefore did not renew their subscriptions.

The fact that they would have made money following his advice was irrelevant. They could not take his advice because they found it psychologically impossible to do so. How can you believe a man who tells you that the market is going to fall when everyone else is telling you what you really want to hear—that it is going to keep going up? No one has a hope of being believed unless he tells people what confirms their own prejudices. All successful persuaders from the serpent in the Garden of Eden to the greatest mob orator, Hitler, capitalized on this fact. My friend had to stop publishing his market letter because no one wanted to hear his views, correct though they were.

I have a broker who has similar incurable hang-ups and prejudices. He has seen me make a fortune in the market and he knows the method I use but he does not believe what he sees. According to him I am doing all the wrong things. He believes in buying cheap stock, selling it if it goes up a couple of points, holding on and averaging down if the price falls, and never selling anything that shows a loss. In short, he does exactly the opposite of everything I do. He is convinced that I must be using some form of trickery and that I will come a cropper some day. Meanwhile I go on making money and he is left with "cats and dogs" in his portfolio.

It is part of the herd instinct to follow the crowd, accept conventional wisdom, and do what everyone else is doing. That is why rational, conservative, level-headed businessmen who would never make a business or financial decision or take any step involving investment in their business without a thorough investigation often throw caution to the winds and buy a stock or mere gossip and hearsay in a bull market. When all your fellow lemmings are rushing into the sea what chance does an isolated lemming have of remaining unaffected by the craze? When stocks are soaring and everyone seems to be making money easily and effortlessly how can even the most intelligent resist the temptation to jump on the bandwagon? The craze is so infectious that having a superior intellect is no protection against it—doctors, lawyers, accountants, and the intellectual elite seem even more vulnerable than the rest of us when the market is in full cry.

Many investors become so emotionally involved with the market that they come to regard it as an adversary with whom, if they cannot beat it, they must at least get even. A business acquainance of mine once bought a stock at 18, saw it rise to 44, then drop to 4 and then rise to 17 and drop again. I have told him many times to sell at 17—after all, what is a loss of a point? But no—he refuses to sell it until it reaches his purchase price of 18. He is determined to teach that damn stock a lesson and get even with it. He has now been holding it for ten years waiting for that opportunity! The stock's price is now 9 and it shows no sign of ever reaching 18.

People's emotions inhibit their stock-market actions in all sorts of curious ways. Many people hesitate to cut their losses on a stock because they are ashamed of looking a fool in the eyes of their broker.

They are too embarrassed to ring him and sell out something which they only recently bought and is declining. Actually, the broker couldn't care less. He is basically interested in turnover, not in whether you have made a mistake or not. He is often *not even aware of it*.

Brokers, in fact, suffer from similar inhibitions. A broker who has recommended that you buy a stock at 20 cannot bring himself to tell you to sell it, as he should, if it immediately declines to 17, because he cannot bear to admit to you that he has made a mistake. Instead he will feed you with comforting statements like "It will come back," "It's just a temporary reaction," "Don't panic," etc., while you watch your stock decline to 10, after which it is "too late" to do anything.

Practically everyone in the stock market seems to put their hopes, fears, inhibitions, vanity, and prejudices before rational thought. How can they possibly succeed?

I am not claiming smugly that I am above all this. I am just as human as anyone. Indeed, as far as stocks are concerned I am the biggest coward on God's earth and I am always ready to run at the slightest sign of trouble. I allow myself to panic because I have learned that I will panic later anyway!

Nevertheless, the extraordinary irrationality of my fellow men, as revealed by their behavior in the stock market, continues to fascinate me. Above all, the "madness of the mind" that contaminates people whenever they are bitten by the "get-rich-quick" bug is a truly remarkable psychological phenomenon. I have never really fathomed it nor have I ever seen any convincing explanation of it, but the realization that it exists and that I am just as prone to it as anyone forced me to take steps to suppress and overcome it. Bitter experience taught me that I could not possibly win in the market if I allowed emotion to influence my decisions. So one of the first steps I took was to keep well away from the marketplace and insulate myself from its ever-changing moods.

So while I continue to trade on Wall Street I keep the market and its emotional atmosphere at arm's length. I do not want to know what people on Wall Street are thinking or saying. I am not interested in the latest business forecasts, analysts' opinions, brokers' views, or tipsters' gossip. The stock tables tell me everything I need to know. It is *what stocks are doing* and *not what people are saying* that determine my actions. This has for a long time been the cornerstone of my market approach and remains so today.

Chapter Six

Although I had parted company with National Semiconductor at a substantial profit that was certainly not the end of my involvement with it. I continued to remain intensely interested in its behavior. I could never really lose interest in the stocks I have successfully traded in the past. Even now, many years later, I still glance at them to see how they are faring, whether they have fallen on bad times, whether they have had a facelift and are attempting to make a comeback like an aged movie star, or whether they have all but gone to their eternal rest. It is difficult to forget one's close friends (for that is how I thought of them), even though they may now be mere shadows of their former selves.

I therefore continued to watch the behavior of National Semiconductor in case the reaction which had taken me out should turn out to be a temporary one. I was quite prepared to buy it back if it turned round, but I first wanted to see if it could come back to and exceed its previous high of nearly 48. But the price continued to fall precipitously and in a matter of weeks had reached a low of 32. I did not like the look of this drop at all, so even when the price stopped falling and started to rise unevenly again in September I began to suspect that all was not well.

In fact the stock took *four months* to regain the ground it lost in a mere few weeks and seemed to me to be struggling every dollar of the way. I decided that its action was so unconvincing that I would stay out for good. The stock price did eventually reach a new high of 55⅜ in February 1976 but it then ran out of steam. Try as it might it just could not make any further progress. I could almost feel it huffing and puffing as buyers and sellers fought it out around the 50 mark for over two months. I watched fascinated to see who would win.

Gradually the sellers won the upper hand and a slow retreat started, which by June had become almost a rout. In July with the stock around 35 the news came out which explained all. It was announced that delivery of digital watches in the first fiscal half year would be only half what had been anticipated due to problems at the company's Bangkok plant. The shares fell nearly two dollars in one day on a volume of nearly three-quarters of a million shares as luckless holders panicked out of the stock. But it was too late. The stock had been sending out danger signals months before as knowledgeable insiders got out and distributed their stock to willing but less knowledgeable buyers. *This* had been the reason for the stock's hesitation after its initial rise! The writing had been on the wall for those whose eyes were sharp enough to see it. My decision to clear out and stay out had been vindicated.

In some ways the behavior of the share price was even more reliable than inside information. If someone had whispered to me that he had heard from an "unimpeachable source" that National Semiconductor was having production troubles I would not have known whether to believe him or not. Was the information true or false, reliable or planted, solidly based or completely unfounded? There was no way in which I or any other outsider like me could have found out with certainty. But I did not need to—the behavior of the stock told me all I wanted to know.

I had no idea of course that the company was having troubles at its plant. My actions had been governed purely by the behavior of the stock in the market. *I had behaved like an insider without actually being one!*

An insider with privileged information only has an advantage so long as he doesn't act on it. As soon as he acts on his information the ticker tape reveals his knowledge and he loses his advantage. True, I had not sold at the top any more than I had bought at the bottom. But I had made a wonderful profit in a matter of months and got out before trouble came. I had no reason to feel dissatisfied with my performance.

Curiously enough, logical, straightforward and effective though my approach to the stock was, many people to whom I talked about it refused to accept that it was a valid and workable means of investing profitably in the market. I once had a very good friend who is a wealthy, respected, and successful businessman. He also like to dabble in the stock market. He goes about it with painstaking thoroughness, analyzing likely companies to the *n*th degree, going through company balance sheets with a fine toothcomb and an electronic calculator, and never making an investment without detailed financial investigation. His ability to analyze and appreciate the minutest detail of a company's financial state would make any accountant green with envy.

The interesting thing about my friend though was that despite his undoubted business acumen and his uncanny ability to grasp financial matters he never made any money in the stock market. On the contrary, he made every mistake in the book. You name it, he did it. He consistently bought at the top and sold at the bottom, he got locked into unsalable stock, he constantly misjudged every move of the market—and he lost half his income every year.

I often tried to help him to improve his performance but he refused to listen to me. He was convinced that his approach was correct and that it was the market that was perverse. The fact that I had made a fortune using my methods and he had made nothing but mistakes cut no ice with him. He believed in earnings, intrinsic value, return on capital, etc., as the determinants of share prices and nothing I said could convince him otherwise. If the market refused to agree with him so much the worse for the market. Meanwhile he went on losing money.

I attempted many times to explain to him the logic of my method. A company may have the most wonderful fundamentals in the world, I said, but if people do not buy the company's stock its share price will not go up one cent. Similarly, what is the point of buying a stock that is "cheap" if it then proceeds to get cheaper? But he turned a deaf ear to my arguments.

My technique of buying a stock only when it has penetrated through the top of its topmost box and the precaution of simultaneously protecting my initial buy with a close stop-loss also seems difficult for many people to swallow, despite the fact that it is based purely on observation of how share prices actually behave. Stock-brokers in particular seem to suffer from a peculiar mental blockage regarding it. I was once interested in a stock that was bobbing about in a 12–16 box. I gave my broker an order to buy it if it went to 16¼ and to sell it if it subsequently dropped to 15. (At the time I gave the order the stock was selling at 14.) My broker thought that he hadn't heard me correctly. "Surely, Mr. Darvas, you mean I should *buy* the stock at 15 and *sell* it at 16¼, not the other way round as you said. And in any case why should I wait to buy it at 16¼ when I can buy it more cheaply for you right now at 14?" Try as I might

I just could not get him to understand that my original
instructions were correct and that I was not out of my
mind. As far as he was concerned shares are like oranges
—why buy them for six cents when you can get them
for four cents?

As it turned out the price of the stock never reached
16¼. After rising to 16 it went into reverse and eventually fell away to 10½. If I had bought the stock when
it was going "cheap" at 14 I would have lost a bundle.
So much for bargain stocks.

PART II

Dar•Card©

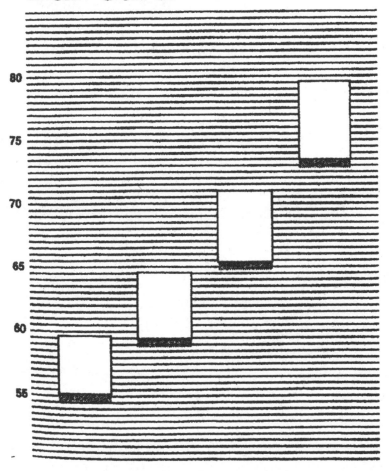

Chapter Seven

I first noticed Moore-McCormack when it appeared in the list of new highs in April 1974. I paid no particular attention to it at the time but merely made a mental note that it was curious that a stock should be hitting new highs at a time when the majority of stocks were falling.

As the market continued to drop and the lists of new lows grew depressingly longer and longer, often running into many hundreds, Moore-McCormack kept popping up in the list of new highs. For example, in the week ending June 28 when 637 stocks on the New York Stock Exchange reached new lows Moore-McCormack was one of only thirteen stocks that hit new highs. I noticed that the stock continued to hit new highs in July and August, often accompanied by enormous spurts in trading volume. I could hardly believe it, but as the market was now dropping precipitously I was too scared to do anything about it anyway. However, when at the end of August Moore-McCormack again reached a new high in a week when no fewer than 1,012 stocks reached new lows I decided to take a closer look at this extraordinary phenomenon.

When I checked up on the company's background I was rather disappointed to find that there was nothing particularly exciting about it. The company provided cargo liner services, bulk transportation, managed mining properties, and sold coal. What could be more uninteresting? A forward-looking space-age industry? Forget it! I was tempted to drop it there and then but I continued to remain fascinated by its extraordinary strength compared with other stocks. By October the price had risen all the way from 12⅜ to over 34, hitting new highs all along the way.

This is too much, I thought to myself. Damn the background, the fundamentals, the industry; there must be *some* reason for this remarkable behavior. There's no smoke without fire—perhaps Moore-McCormack has developed a new supersonic cargo ship, I conjectured ruefully.

But just as I was becoming sufficiently interested to consider buying it, the market, fickle as ever, dropped the stock more than ten points to 23 in December. I was just about ready to kiss the stock good-bye when to my astonishment it rose back up to 30 in January 1975 and continued on its upward march.

By now I was really on the alert. There was something going on here, I was certain. A stock doesn't come up from 12 to 34, drop to near 20, and then quickly rise to over 30 again for no good reason. I neither knew nor cared what the reasons were. *This stock was a buy on its technical action alone!* I resolved to go into it if it rose above its previous high.

I didn't have to wait long. At the beginning of February Moore-McCormack broke out swiftly from a narrow 33–32 box and I bought a block of shares at 34½. I had hardly managed to get my order in when the stock took off in a phenomenal fashion. By the end of February it had gone over 45, by the first week of April it was over 55, and by the beginning of May it was touching 70! What was going on—had Moore-McCormack discovered a means of transporting coal to Mars?

This can't last, I told myself. I was ready to make a mad dash for the exit at the first sign of trouble. But Moore-McCormack just kept on soaring—75—79—85—90! I watched breathless, almost hypnotized. I had never seen anything quite like it. This was a stock straight out of Alice in Wonderland—it was now jumping 5 to 7 points a day! Where would it all end? I was more and more on the alert. I have never moved a stop-loss up faster. I hardly had time to think, let alone act.

I knew this could not go on much longer. I was determined to hold on to the stock as long as it kept rising, but my hand was on the rip cord of my stop-loss parachute ready to jump clear when the first reaction came. This was certainly not a stock you could put away and forget about! On July 23 Moore-McCormack reached a phenomenal high of 95⅜—and then the bottom dropped out. On July 29 the stock dropped over nine points; on July 31 it dropped a further seven points. Air pockets appeared on all sides—I have never seen a stock fall to earth so quickly. I sold out at 85 and then watched, almost unable to believe my eyes, as it fell away to 53 in a mere two weeks. My ejector seat had thrown me clear just in time. If I had held on even a few days longer I would have lost another twenty points.

This story had an interesting sequel. About a year later while I was staying in Paris I got into conversation with an American tourist who happened to be sitting next to me in my hotel. In due course our talk turned to the stock market and I mentioned to him my remarkable experience with Moore-McCormack. "Oh yes," he said, "the company had an interest in a mining venture in northwestern Quebec with promising deposits of copper, zinc, and silver minerals. That's what all the excitement was about." "Why did the stock collapse?" I asked him. "The company announced in July," he explained, "that third-quarter earnings would be down on those of the previous year." I looked skeptical. "Does a mere 'interest' in a mine in Canada merit a rise in stock price from 12 to 95, and does a forecast of reduced earnings justify a price fall of nearly 50 percent?" I asked him. He shrugged, "Probably not," he conceded, "but that's the nature of the stock-market animal. Ours is not to reason why."

I told him that I had bought Moore-McCormack on

Dar·Card ©

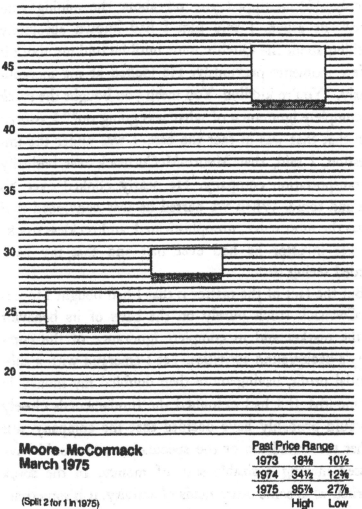

Moore-McCormack
March 1975

(Split 2 for 1 in 1975)

51

the way up at 34½ and sold it on the way down at 85 just before the stock collapsed. He looked at me enviously, "Who tipped you off about the mining venture?" he asked. I told him I had known absolutely nothing about the Quebec mine until he told me about it a few moments previously. He looked at me incredulously. "You're kidding. You mean you bought the stock in complete ignorance of what was going on?" I assured him that that was in fact the case. I was under the impression, I said, that Moore-McCormack was basically a transportation company. He nearly choked over his gin and tonic. When we parted he was convinced that I was the most naive, unsophisticated, and reckless stock-market investor he had ever met and that my head needed seeing to.

But the fact of the matter is that I had bought Moore-McCormack stock purely on the basis of its behavior in the market and in complete ignorance of the company's background activities. Yet I emerged with a substantial profit, having more than doubled my money in six months. If I had examined the fundamentals closely I would probably have decided that the company was either too humdrum or too speculative and would have missed making a sizable sum of money. In the stock market, as in some other fields of activity, it is sometimes better not to know too much.

Chapter Eight

In my talks with people about the stock market I was surprised to find that many of them felt that they no longer stood any chance whatever of making money in stocks. "The market is now completely dominated by the institutions," I was told again and again. "The big institutional money has taken control. The era of the small man is over." Is it true? If it is, I and every other private investor like me are wasting our time and money buying stocks. However, when we look at the facts we find that the truth is quite the opposite of what is generally believed.

The idea that we are pitting our wits against the big institutions and therefore don't stand a chance is based on a complete misunderstanding of the aims and attitudes of the institutions. The institutions are not interested in making big money or "beating the market." They are primarily interested in a safe, steady income. When the performance bubble of the Sixties burst it left behind many burned fingers and broken careers, so the emphasis now is all on solidity, safety and, hopefully, an average return of 9 percent per annum. Thus the institutions are not interested in finding growth stocks and making big capital gains. They are more concerned in trying to determine which way the market as a whole is going to move. Once they have convinced themselves that the market is going to go up they simply buy a selection of well-known blue chips. They leave the up-and-coming growth stocks severely alone. They regard them as "too speculative."

Unimaginative though such action may see, they do not really have much choice. They have such enormous sums to invest that they are forced to pick companies with large blocks of stock outstanding. An institution with $500 million to invest cannot invest it in a company with only two million shares outstanding. An even greater problem arises when it comes to selling stock. How does an institution sell $10 million worth of a stock in a falling market? The answer is that very often it can't. Ten million dollars worth of stock cannot be sold like $10,000 worth. Thus the institutions usually have no choice but to sit on their portfolios through thick and thin. Hence their rather unexciting performance.

The institutional manager's nightmare is to buy an unknown stock which he feels has big growth prospects, see its price drop to zero overnight, and have to explain and justify his action to the board of diretcors. So he plays safe, buys U.S. Steel, IBM, Exxon, ITT, and the like and sits on them for at least five years if not forever.

He argues that if he buys ITT no one can accuse him of
being a reckless impetuous gambler, even if the price of
ITT falls 50 percent. So he's covered. And of course
ITT looks good on the institution's portfolio of stocks.
It's solid, safe, comforting, and dividend-paying. Never
mind if the stock is standing at way below its purchase
price. That's just unfortunate; no one can blame *him*
for it.

The private investor like myself and the institutions
are thus completely different animals. Our aims and
objects are poles apart. I would never in a hundred years
buy the stocks the institutions buy, so I never feel that I
am fighting an unequal battle with them. They have
their objectives and I have mine. They buy and sell their
stocks and I buy and sell mine. We live in different
worlds. Our activities are quite independent and I certainly never feel that I am being pushed around or dominated by them. On the contrary, I feel rather sorry for
them in that they are forced to operate within such rigid
constraints while I am free to do more or less as I wish.

Can the private investor still make it in the market?
My experience with Moore-McCormack shows that he
certainly can. What is more, he has a number of factors
in his favor. Firstly, he has agility and flexibility, that is,
he can switch from one stock to another rapidly, and
can buy and sell stock at any time without much difficulty. The institutions, because of their large holdings,
cannot buy, sell, or switch with anything like the ease of

the smaller investor. Secondly, he can remain completely liquid for long periods when the market is in a down trend and it is best to own no stocks at all. The institutions generally have to remain at least partially invested whatever the market climate and very often find themselves locked in anyway. Thirdly, the small investor can invest in the smaller second-line companies with greater growth potential and he does not need to diversify to any great extent. He can thus concentrate on three or four promising stocks instead of diluting his capital among a large number of diverse holdings (as the institutions do) and hence obtaining only average results. So, astonishing though it may seem, the private investor's chances of making money in the market are even better than the institution's.

The institutions, it is true, have formidable investment hardware at their disposal—computers, sophisticated statistical data, the latest information, and the best advice. Despite all these apparent advantages they are still as fallible as they ever were. In 1972 over one hundred financial institutions were asked to name their favorite stocks for 1973. If you had invested equal amounts in their recommended stocks you would have lost over 40 percent of your money in the following twelve months. For all their expensive equipment the institutions can still make expensive mistakes. (Much the same result, incidentally, was obtained in a similar survey carried out way back in 1932. Plus ça change, plus c'est la même chose—the more things change, the more they stay the same, as the saying goes.)

If the small investor has deserted the stock market it is not because the institutions have crowded him out but because he has suffered such devastating losses in the last two bear markets that he has become disillusioned. In the circumstances it is only human nature to try to find a scapegoat, and the institutions provide a convenient target to blame for his misfortune. Yet this need never have happened if people had taken the simple advice I gave over fifteen years ago—*never enter the market without protecting yourself against loss.*

My advice now is just as simple and straightforward as it was then: *when you buy a stock keep in the forefront of your mind, not the great killing you are going to make, but the possibility that your stock could drop 50 percent in value very quickly.* Never ever let this happen to you. *Set a stop-loss, even if only a mental one, such that you sell out any stock that has dropped 20 percent below its highest price.* With these simple precautions you will never suffer huge losses in a bear market, holding stock will never become a nightmare, and you can forget about the institutions.

Chapter Nine

The well-known American physicist Richard Feynman once likened the scientist to an observer watching two men playing chess inside a glass enclosure. The observer does not know what the game is all about and cannot hear what the players say. All he can do is watch the players from the outside. After a while, however, he is able to deduce the rules of the game and hence forecast the winner.

My approach to the market is much the same. I watch stocks, see how they move, and pick out those whose behavior marks them out as future winners.

But the scientist can sometimes misinterpret what he sees due to wishful thinking, prejudgment, lack of care, or by overlooking some vitally important detail. In the same way it is possible to *misinterpret* a stock's moves and end up picking a stock that does not behave as you thought it would. That can't be helped. There's no sure thing in the market—that is why you must *always* have a stop-loss. Having made a mistake the obvious thing to do is to clear out, lick one's wounds, and look for another stock. Logical and sensible though this may seem, on certain occasions, against all reason, I have compounded my initial mistake by coming back for more punishment and emerged at the end of it all bruised, battered, and badly mauled, wondering ruefully why I took leave of my senses. One of my most traumatic and painful experiences was with Hughes Tool.

"The stocks that go up first in a bull market are the stocks to buy"—how often I have heard that said! It is almost one of the market's ten commandments. No doubt it is often true, but "often" isn't good enough to give you a sure profit. Even if it is true 99 percent of the time that 1 percent margin of error can be enough to cause disaster. So it was with me.

When watching the market in the fall of 1974 I noticed Hughes Tool rise from a low of around 36 in September to around 72 in November—although the market averages were still falling. During the same period Houston Oil and Minerals (quoted on the American Stock Exchange) rose from around 12½ to over 32. So a month later when the whole market turned round and started rising there was no doubt in my mind that these must be the stocks to buy. If they could double in the months before the bull market began they must surely soar when the bull market really got into its stride. I happened to be in New York at the time (a fatal mistake as it turned out), so my broker was right at hand. I could hardly wait. This was a cinch, I told myself.

I picked up the phone and confidently gave my broker instructions to buy Hughes Tool at 73 with a stop-loss of 71½. The stock was duly bought for me—and three days later I was sold out! The stock had dipped to 69. I was dumbfounded. I was sure this was the right stock but no sooner had I stepped in the front door than it unceremoniously threw me out the window.

Any prudent man having received a bloody nose from the "bouncer" at the door would have had the sense to keep away. But not me! This was a fabulously strong stock, I told myself, so strong it had already doubled so it must go up further now that confidence has returned to the market. I would try again.

I dusted myself down and told my broker to buy it again at 73¼ with a stop-loss of 71½. Once more the stock was bought for me—and once again within a matter of days I was sold out!

I have learned from experience that there are some stocks I just cannot handle, so after two unsuccessful bites at the cherry, chipping my teeth on the stone in the process, I would normally leave them severely alone. But not this time. I was so hypnotized by the early strong behavior of this stock that I could not leave it alone. I threw caution to the winds. I didn't wait for anything, boxes, penetrations, volume, nothing. Every time it rose I bought—and was sold out each time a few days later. I was constantly on the telephone to my broker, going up and down with Hughes Tool like an elevator boy.

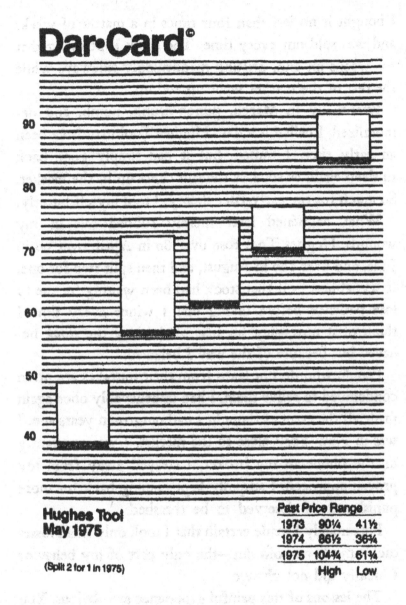

Dar•Card©

Hughes Tool
May 1975

(Split 2 for 1 in 1975)

Past Price Range		
1973	90¼	41½
1974	86½	36¼
1975	104¼	61¼
	High	Low

I bought it no less than four times in a matter of weeks and was sold out every time. The stock kept doing that for weeks on end, drifting maddeningly sideways while the rest of the market went up and up.

Eventually in March, punch-drunk, numb, and demoralized, I called it a day. Hughes Tool may have been an early riser, I mused, but it had simply gone back to sleep again as soon as the sun came up in the market. So much for the early-riser theory, I told myself bitterly.

What happened later merely rubbed salt in my wounds. Hughes Tool rose over 80 in April, over 90 in June, and over 100 in August, and then split two for one. It was almost as if that stock had been waiting for me to lose patience before taking off! I wince every time I think of it now—not because of the way the *stock* behaved but because of the way *I* behaved.

People who do not learn from their mistakes are often condemned to relive them. I had unbelievably once again made all the errors I thought I had outgrown years ago. I was in New York close to the market, I was constantly on the phone to my broker, I strayed away from my proven approach, I stupidly kept coming back for more punishment. I deserved to be thrashed.

Fortunately I made certain that I took only small losses each time I was sold out—the only part of my behavior I luckily did not change.

The lessons of this painful experience are obvious. You must have some system, some rules of behavior when you

buy stocks. Any system is better than none at all. And
everyone must include a stop-loss. To enter the market
without some rules or to abandon those rules in mid-
stream for no good reason is like setting out to sea in a
boat with no rudder. You drift aimlessly at the mercy
of the tide and wind and eventually and inevitably sink.

Chapter Ten

After nearly trebling in value, from around 11 to 32½, in a mere two months between September and November 1974 Houston Oil and Minerals had quietly gone to sleep. While I was wrestling with Hughes Tool and getting the worst of it I kept a watchful eye on Houston Oil to see whether it was just pausing for breath prior to another dramatic upsurge or whether the show was now over and I had missed my opportunity. Having been taught a lesson by Hughes Tool I was determined not to make a fool of myself a second time. This time I would be patient, watchful, careful, keep strictly to my method, and not jump the gun.

But Houston Oil was equal to it. It just lay there month after month after month and did nothing. It was almost as if it knew what my intentions were and was determined to give me a run for my money. Throughout the whole of 1974 Houston Oil and I just stared coldly at one another, each of us waiting for the other to make the first move. We were like the outlaw and the sheriff facing each other at opposite ends of Main Street, each with his hands hovering over his Colt forty-fives, waiting for the other to draw. The stock's high was 32 ½ and I decided that I would not move until that top was penetrated substantially.

By October I had been waiting for over six months and still nothing had happened. Most people would have given up by this time, written the stock off as a has-been, and transferred their attention elsewhere. But to me waiting is just another form of activity. It is an essential part of my stock-market armory. Ability to sit and wait for the right opportunity to arrive is a necessary requirement for success. I sensed that Houston Oil, like Hughes Tool, was just waiting for me to lose patience before breaking out of its box. It was going to stretch my patience to the breaking point and then shoot just as soon as I turned my back on it. This was going to be a real battle of wits, patience, and tactics.

In the middle of October the stock moved up to 32 ⅛, as if tempting me into buying too soon in anticipation of a breakout. I itched to do so. I had been waiting for this breakout for so long that my money was practically burning a hole in my pocket. But I held back and in the next few days the price dropped back again. I was really on my guard now. Houston Oil was playing with me, I could sense it. It was as if that damn stock knew that I had made a fool of myself with Hughes Tool and was going to try and make me do the same again. I could hardly believe my eyes. I was being taunted and tempted into making mistakes!

Suddenly, in the second week of November the price jumped to 32⅞—a mere ⅜ above the top of its box. This would normally have been the signal for me to buy, but I knew this stock now and I decided to hold back and wait for a more positive penetration. I would not go for my gun just yet. How right I was! The stock dropped back below the top of the box again and in the following weeks never went above 27–28. If I had bought it at the first penetration I would have been stopped out in a matter of days just as I had been with Hughes Tool. I smiled grimly to myself. First round to me, I thought, I felt instinctively that I had got the measure of this stock. It had tried to tease me, mislead me, outsit me, and outsmart me and had failed. I sensed that the shooting was now about to start.

I was right. In the middle of January 1976, well over a year after its initial rise, Houston Oil rose strongly to 34¾. This was it! I rushed an order to my broker to buy 800 shares at the market with a 10 percent stop-loss. Meanwhile, the price established itself in a 33–35½ box, followed at the beginning of February by a new 35–40 box. My stop-loss was not touched off. Within a couple of weeks the price was touching 45 and by March, after a five-for-four split, had reached the equivalent of 50.

I was walking on air. I had won! My long tedious wait,

my eyeball-to-eyeball confrontation with the stock had
paid off. Only two months after buying it the price was
already 50 percent above what I had paid for it. Two
months later, when the stock rose into a 54–63 box, I had
all but doubled my money. It had been worth the long
wait. (At the time of writing it had passed 70, equivalent
to 87½ before the adjustment for the five-for-four split.)

Houston Oil restored my confidence after the beating
I had received from Hughes Tool. It also revealed to me
more clearly something that I had been dimly aware
of in the past and that is—*you must know your stock.*
By that I don't mean that you must know the company,
its products, its history, etc. I mean literally that you
must know the personality of the stock you are buying,
its idiosyncrasies, its moods, its mode of behavior. This
may seem far-fetched but the fact is that two stocks can
be as different as chalk and cheese in their market action
even though they may be virtually identical in every
other respect. Some are slow, lethargic, and almost
apathetic. Others are volatile, fidgety, and nervous and
jump at the slightest happening.

I had become familiar with Houston Oil and its behavior over a period of many years and I knew what a
tricky customer it could be. My knowledge of the stock
based on observation of its past behavior enabled me to
keep one step ahead at every stage. This intimacy was the
weapon that I used to emerge the victor.

Dar·Card°

Houston Oil and Minerals
July 1976

(Split 2 for 1 in 1973
Split 2 for 1 in 1974)

Past Price Range		
1973	68⅞	28½
1974	32½	11⅝
1975	32	19⅞
	High	Low

Chapter Eleven

It was just like the good old days!! I once again felt the exhilaration I first felt in the Fifties when I watched my first "Darvas" stocks soaring to unbelievable heights. Houston Oil gave me the boost I needed at that moment. I had not lost my flair; I could still tussle with stocks and come out on top.

After my first book was published many people wrote and told me that I had just been plain lucky. I had come into the market in the booming Fifties when all sorts of new and exciting stocks were being born. I had arrived during the "electronics" era when innumerable stocks in this field went up practically tenfold—stocks like Texas Instruments, Fairchild Camera, and Zenith Radio. I hadn't really been particularly smart, it seemed, I had just had the good fortune to be in the right place at the right time. Those days are over, I was repeatedly told. Would I have the same "lucky breaks" in the volatile Seventies that I apparently had in the soaring Fifties?

But those days are not over! There are always "Darvas" stocks around. There is never a shortage of exciting opportunities to make big money in the market. The electronics and space age didn't end in the Fifties—it's still here. There is no limit to man's versatility and inventiveness. Electronics was followed by computers, semiconductors, lasers, missiles, satellites, and the most sophisticated gadgetry imaginable. As lang as there are discoveries, developments, fads, and fashions there will always be "Darvas" stocks. The art is to find them in their early stages and get aboard in time to ride them up. They are there just waiting to be discovered.

Finding such stocks is not like looking for the pro-verbial needle in a haystack; they are sending out "bleeps" all the time to be picked up by the antennae of the observant market watcher. Sudden rises in price and volume, out of the ordinary relative strength, and move-ment against the general market trend are all giveaway signals which reveal the presence of a stock about to take off.

Even while Houston Oil and I were glaring at each other from opposite corners of the ring I did not give up my daily routine of scouring the stock-market tables for promising stocks. I habitually spend at least half an hour a day doing this. I regard it as absolutely essential. It is only by such regular scanning of the stock tables that one can train one's eyes to observe significant changes. When your eyes have become familiar with the arrangement of the furniture in a room you can quickly spot when some rearrangement has occurred.

In the closing days of September 1976 the market suddenly collapsed. As usual, it took everyone completely by surprise. The market had been yo-yoing up and down through the 1,000 mark on the Dow throughout most of 1976, unable to make any headway. Suddenly it broke out—upwards, reaching a new three-and-a-half-year high on a volume of thirty million shares, giving all the appearances of having snapped out of its lethargy at last. But it was just another of the market's cruel tricks—a classic bull trap. Within a matter of weeks the index had dropped over eighty points to a nine-month low, catching investors completely off guard. After feinting with its right the market had caught investors with a straight left, leaving them stunned, punch-drunk, groggy, and stupefied from the unexpectedness of it all.

So the bull market that had begun so dramatically and surprisingly in the fall of 1974 ended equally dramatically and unexpectedly in the fall of 1976. When it did I was holding just three stocks—Houston Oil (bought at 34, now at 70 after a five-for-four split), Teledyne (bought at 27½, now 68), and Mitchell Energy and Development (bought at 27, now 41)—all of them fitted with protective stop-losses to guard against just such a market reversal. However, my stocks held up remarkably well, remaining close to their year's highs, despite the weak market.

I was showing a handsome profit from this two-year

bull market, with all its surprises, trials, dilemmas, and frustrations. But what gave me even more satisfaction was the knowledge that I had once again found "Darvas" stocks. Just another "lucky break"? Perhaps, but the method I had used was no different from the one I first used some twenty years ago when I had my original "lucky breaks." I merely bought strong stocks in developing industries in a rising market and protected myself at every stage against a possible downturn. It was as simple as that. Luck may have played a part but as far as I am concerned my success was due entirely to my systematic approach, married to an innate caution based on experience. Markets, companies, products, governments, and even the economy itself may change but there is no doubt in my mind that there will always be "Darvas" stocks waiting for the sharp-eyed investor to discover. You can still make it in the market!

Chapter Twelve

In the Hotel George V in Paris where I have lived for some thirty years I have two good friends, Mr. Falcucci, the hotel manager, and Mr. Klein, the director of reception. From time to time we get together in the lounge for a drink and a chat. One evening when we were having one of our quiet discussions Mr. Falcucci quite out of the blue, suddenly said to me, "I understand you are writing another book on the stock market."

I had been questioning various guests about their stock-market problems and experiences so I assumed that the word must have got around.

"Yes, 'that's right," I replied, "at the moment I'm just gathering material for it."

"I would be very interested to hear your views on my portfolio," he said.

I sat up astonished. This was the first I'd heard of Mr. Falcucci mixing stocks with hotel management. It hadn't occurred to me to ask him about *his* stock-market experiences.

"I had no idea you owned stocks. Why didn't you mention it to me before?" I asked.

"I had often thought of asking your advice about my stocks but somehow it slipped my mind."

"Stocks should never slip your mind; you should keep your eye on them all the time."

"Well, I have other things to think about. I just put my stocks in the bottom drawer and assumed that they would look after themselves and eventually provide me with a nest egg to retire on."

"How do you come to have these stocks? What made you buy them?"

"Oh, rich Americans passing through often gave me stock-market tips. Whatever they recommended I should buy, I bought," he replied.

By now I was all ears. "I would be fascinated to see what you have acquired over the years. Could you let me see a list of your holdings?"

"Certainly," he replied happily. "Let's meet here to-morrow night and discuss it."

"It's a date."

While we were engaged in these exchanges Mr. Klein had been listening with rapt attention without saying anything. He suddenly interjected. "Can I bring my portfolio along as well?' he asked.

I was taken aback. "What, you too!" I exclaimed.

"Yes, I have also built up a portfolio of stocks in the same way over many years. I would also be grateful for your advice."

"Well, bring it along tomorrow night too," I said.

It was past midnight when we shook hands and they departed, leaving me to my thoughts. What a coincidence, I thought to myself. The manager and director of reception of one of the most fashionable and cosmopolitan hotels in the world with portfolios of stocks recommended by some of the richest people in the United States! What would they be like—a dull list of safe conservative blue chips, a worthless collection of cats and dogs, or an Ali Baba's cave of some of the greatest stocks in history? It could be sensational. I could hardly wait for the next evening to arrive.

When we met the following evening I was tense with excitement. Both Mr. Falcucci and Mr. Klein had had their portfolios typed out on sheets of paper with the date of purchase indicated for each stock. I glanced through them quickly. My first impression as I scanned the long lists of stocks was the large number of holdings they had. Each list contained nearly twenty stocks.

This was diversification gone mad.

"Why did you buy so many stocks?" I asked in astonishment.

"For safety," they replied. Our clients advised us, they told me, to invest in a large number of stocks in order to "spread the risk."

I tried to explain to them that this was bad advice and showed a complete misunderstanding of the nature of stocks. In practice, I said, the only risk diversification guards you against is the remote possibility that one of the companies whose stock you have bought will go bankrupt. In a bear market diversification provides no protection whatsoever—practically all stocks with few exceptions will decline.

To make matters worse, diversification has serious disadvantages, I told them. Firstly, by spreading your money over a large number of stocks you merely ensure that you will get only average results at best, since in any portfolio the big profits generally come from only a small number of stocks. The others serve no useful purpose and merely drag the performance down.

Both Mr. Falcucci and Mr. Klein expressed surprise at this view.

"Surely you are not suggesting that we should put all our money into just two or three stocks?"

"No, of course not," I said, "there is nothing wrong with making a 'pilot' buy of all the stocks you were recommended. But that should not be the end of the matter."

I explained that having bought a large collection of stocks the correct procedure then was to sell those that declined, stagnated, or did not perform as expected and reinvest the money in those that *did* perform by going up.

"I have usually found that the strong get stronger and the weak get weaker," I said.

"Secondly, you are both busy men, so how can you possibly keep an eye on so many stocks?" I asked. "Some of them could fall to zero without you even being aware of it."

They admitted that this had not occurred to them. After all, they said, the stocks had been recommended by the best people.

"There's no sure thing in the market," I replied. "Despite the most painstaking analysis, the most reliable information, and no matter how impeachable the source, stocks have the annoying habit of doing exactly the opposite of what you expect. The price of safety is eternal vigilance, if I may adapt a phrase. You must keep a constant eye on your stocks. That is why a small portfolio is essential."

I drew an analogy with a class of unruly kids. The discipline is likely to be much better in a class of five, I said, than in a class of thirty. If one of the class misbehaves the teacher can see straightaway who the offender is and take remedial action. If anyone in a class of thirty starts to misbehave the teacher hardly knows whom to deal with first.

"I know my stocks are going to start playing up sooner or later so, paradoxical though it may seem, the fewer I have the safer I feel. This is one case where there is certainly not safety in numbers," I said laughing.

It slowly began to dawn on Mr. Falcucci and Mr. Klein that there was more to stock investment than just giving an order to a broker and writing out a check.

"But I would be very reluctant to put all my money

into two or three stocks," mused Mr. Klein. "That seems to me to be a very very risky idea."

Mr. Falcucci agreed. "I would be extremely scared if I thought all my money was hanging on the fate of a couple of stocks. I wouldn't be able to sleep at night."

"You are quite right to think that way," I replied. "If you think I've got nerves of steel you are wrong. A bigger coward than I in the stock market has not yet been born. That is why I developed the stop-loss to such a fine art."

I had to explain to them what a stop-loss was.

"No stock keeps going up for ever," I pointed out. "As they say on Wall Street, 'No tree grows to the sky.' A stock might be in an uptrend today but there is no way of knowing when the uptrend will cease and go into reverse. Since I found out early in my stock-market career that failure to sell a falling stock is one of the main reasons for poor investment results, I long ago adopted an automatic safety mechanism for selling me out of any stock that did not appear to be behaving properly. I simply instructed my broker in advance to sell me out if the price of my stock fell below a certain level. This freed me from the dilemma of when to sell. My stop-loss made the decision for me and I lost no sleep worrying about it."

I was also going to mention that the stop-loss had another enormous advantage which made me resolve never to be without it—it got me out of bear markets quickly before serious losses occurred. It was thanks to this strategy of cutting losses fast that I was saved from the ravages of the terrifying bear markets of the Sixties and Seventies. But it occurred to me that Mr. Falcucci and Mr. Klein were probably not even aware that there had been any bear markets! Where unawareness is bliss it is folly to be wise.

"What do you think of the portfolios?" Mr. Klein asked with interest.

"Your portfolios are a good example of the excellence and uselessness of tips," I answered.

Mr. Klein was clearly puzzled by the apparent contradiction in my reply.

"What do you mean?" he asked.

"Practically every single stock in your portfolio would have made you a fortune—if you had bought and sold them at the right time! Unfortunately tips are never given in that way. What usually happens is that someone tells you to buy a certain stock for some reason or another which he thinks is good. But by the time you get the tip the price may have already reached its top and be on the way down. It is then too late to buy and you should keep clear of it. Alternatively, if you buy it on the way up but don't sell it at the right time you could ride it all the way down again and end up back where you started or worse. That's the trouble with tips—the most important bits of information (when to buy and when to sell) are left out. Without that information tips are useless.

"Take Lums, for example. Before its name was changed to Caesar's World it became involved in the franchising craze; its stock was selling at that time at around 20 cents. In five years its price had risen to $300. Later it collapsed to 27. Was Lums a good tip? It depends whether you bought it at $1 or $300. Buying a stock without checking which way it is going is like stepping into an elevator blindfolded—you don't know whether you are going to be taken up or down.

"I knew a taxi driver in Miami who had the misfortune to ride the elevator up and down. He spent every penny he had buying Lums around 20 cents. He held on to the stock all the way up to $300 and became a millionaire. Unfortunately he then held on to it all the way down again and ended up a pauper."

"But surely it is only the really speculative stocks that suffer such violent swings," interjected Mr. Falcucci. "If you buy stocks in the large established companies I would think you could safely put them away and forget about them and know that they will still be flourishing in ten years time."

"In a perfect, unchanging world that might be true," I replied, "but in the world as it is *no* stock can be regarded as that safe. An increase in home or foreign competition, the invention of a new product, a deterioration in a company's cash situation—all these and many other factors can have a devastating effect on the 'safest' of companies, with serious consequences for the share price. The stock market is littered with the bones of 'quality' companies which just sank into oblivion with the onward march of progress. You could fill a book with the names of them. No, I would never put any shares away no matter how well established the company might seem."

Mr. Klein interrupted, "OK, but we're not talking about companies going bankrupt or 'fad' companies. We mean companies like IBM, Xerox, or Polaroid which have practically no rivals anywhere in the world. Aren't such stocks as steady as a rock?"

"Logically you'd think they would be," I replied, "but the market doesn't follow logic. IBM has been as high as 365 and has fallen as low as 150, the all-time high of Xerox was 172 and it has been as low as 48, and as for Polaroid it has been as high as 149 and as low as 14!"

"But don't they come back up again?"

I shrugged, "There's no law that says they will. Many solid stocks still haven't regained their 1971 level, never mind their 1973 level."

Our mouths were becoming rather dry from all this philosophical discussion. We called the waiter and ordered some beer.

"So what's the solution?" asked Mr. Falcucci.

"There is only one solution. You've just got to keep an eye on your stocks—hold on to them while they are rising, sell them if they decline badly, and *never be married to a stock*. A quick divorce is often cheaper in the long run and less painful." We laughed.

"To be perfectly frank with you," said Mr. Klein, "I don't think I can really be bothered to keep going in and out like that and constantly watching my stocks like a cat watching a mouse. If that's what's required to be successful and even to be safe I'd rather keep my money in the bank."

"Well, not everyone is temperamentally suited to the stock market," I replied. "Anyone who is unwilling or unable to devote some time to it is probably better off out of the game altogether. But since you already own stocks it seems to me to be worth while to try and maximize your profits, and that I'm afraid does necessitate an active and not a passive role."

"What puzzles me," said Mr. Falcucci, blowing a smoke ring, "is why stocks fluctuate so wildly. I don't see how these wild rises and sickening drops can possibly be related to the business activities of the companies concerned. It makes no sense to me at all."

"I also found it very puzzling for many years," I replied. "It's quite common for the share price of a company to go into a steep decline despite the fact that the company has announced increased earnings. Conversely, strange as it may seem, a company with no earnings or

which has not paid a dividend for years may often see
its share price soar.

"One of the stocks in your portfolio was like that—
Great Western United. I remember it attracted my attention in 1974 because it went up from 3 to 31. When
I checked it out I found that the earnings background
was terrible—the company had shown a deficit, and an
increasing one at that, from 1971 to 1973. The company's
interests were in sugar beets, land, and fast food. Nothing
very revolutionary there, either. Yet the price went up
tenfold in a year."

"It seems crazy but surely there must be some logic
in it somewhere," Mr. Klein remarked.

"Well, it only starts to make sense," I replied, "when
you realize that share prices are determined not by company earnings, dividends, assets, etc., as so many people
fondly believe, but by investors' future expectations,
emotions, sentiments, and even wishful thinking. A company in the red and with no earnings can thus find its
share price climbing purely and simply because an im-
provement in its earnings is anticipated in the future,
even though these expectations are never realized. Similarly, a highly profitable company can suffer a drastic fall
in share price if stockholders take the view (whether
correct or not) that the company's future is not so
bright. So I attach very little importance to analysts' calculations that claim to show what a given share is
'worth.' It is what the market *thinks* the share is worth

Dar·Card

**Great Western United
December 1974**

Past Price Range		
1972	19¼	6½
1973	8¼	1½
1974	31¼	3⅛
	High	Low

and not its theoretical worth that determines its price. Whether the market is 'right' or 'wrong' in its conclusion is irrelevant."

"Do you mean that there is often no rational basis for these violent rises and falls?" asked Mr. Falcucci in astonishment.

"That's exactly what I mean," I replied. "If you want a good example just look at mining stocks. Rumors of a uranium, gold, or nickel strike have sent stocks soaring even though the 'mine' in question was nothing more than a hole in the ground with no hope of producing anything for ten years or more. Eventually people came to their senses, the bubble burst, the stock collapsed, and investors crept away sheepishly to nurse their burned fingers."

"Well, at least we had the sense not to buy any mines," said Mr. Klein.

"Mind you," I continued, "I don't want to give the impression that there are *never* good fundamental reasons for buying a certain stock. Sometimes a stock does go up simply because the company is doing well and everybody is aware of it. Take MCA, for example. I knew the chairman of the board, Lew Wasserman, from my early days in show business so I had always kept a benevolent eye on its stock. The company had had something of a checkered history. It was originally a talent agency (they used to be my agents when I was in show business) but then expanded into movie production. Later it was broken up by Robert Kennedy under the antitrust laws and today it is a conglomerate with first-class management.

"MCA really hit the headlines when it produced the film *Jaws*, which grossed $7 million in the first week. In 1974 everyone was talking about its enormous success so it seemed an obvious buy. When I checked on the price behavior of the stock, however, I didn't like it one bit—it was much too erratic. Better leave it alone, I had told myself. But against my better judgment and purely for reasons of sentiment I bought a mere 100 shares at around 72 to see if I could handle it. In two days I was sold out at 64! I lost about $800 and never touched the stock again. There are some friends it's best not to be too involved with. Fundamentally, though, it was an excellent company and many people made money by buying its stock. I just couldn't handle it.

"The market also has fashions and favorite stocks from time to time. Some of the stocks in your portfolio were very fashionable at one time but are only shadows of their former selves now. For example, Champion Homes was one of a number of mobile-home stocks which went through a terrific period of popularity. Then all of a sudden they went out of fashion and the stock collapsed. I think it went from an all-time high of about 26 to less than $2."

Mr. Klein laughed ruefully, "We would probably

Dar•Card®

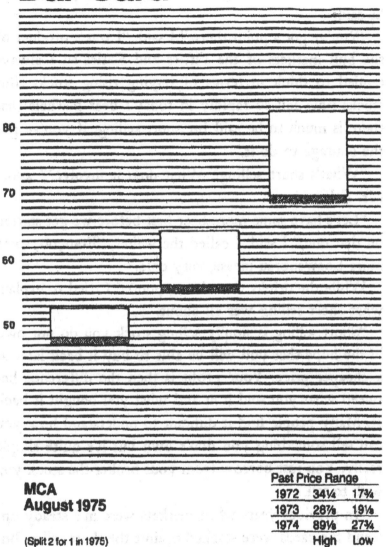

MCA
August 1975

(Split 2 for 1 in 1975)

*8*7

have done better selling them rather than buying them," he said.

"You've got a point there," I said. "I was a product of the bull markets of the Fifties and Sixties so I always tended to think in terms of buying rising stocks. But stocks now fall so rapidly in today's bear markets that there is much to be said for short selling, if you've got the courage to do it."

"What's short selling? What does it involve?" asked Mr. Falcucci.

"Let's have some more beer first before we get started on that one," I said. I called the waiter, "François, some more Loewenbrau please, very cold."

While the drinks were being poured I tried to explain what short selling was all about.

"Short selling is simply selling stock you do not own in the hope that you will be able to buy it back later at a cheaper price. Your profit is then the difference between what you sold it at and what you bought it back at. Many people find it difficult to understand how you can sell something you don't own but it's quite simple really. You just borrow from your broker the stock you wish to sell.

"In previous years when markets were in a steady uptrend the cards were stacked against the short seller. But with the steep bear markets we have been having in the last few years, with the market dropping as much as 50 percent in a mere eighteen months, it now seems to me to be just as logical to sell short in falling markets as to buy in rising markets. I have never done it myself because psychologically I am not cut out for short selling. But I think that markets have now changed their character so much that all experienced investors should seriously consider it. It is not for the proverbial widows and orphans, though."

While I was speaking it suddenly occurred to me that the DAR-CARD could easily be adapted to short selling. All one needed to do was turn the card upside-down so that the red stop-loss area is on *top* of the boxes instead of at the bottom. Hence, when the price rises into the red area, that is the signal to buy the stock back. I was surprised I had not thought of that before.

"Hm, I'm not sure now whether the tips we received were worth having or not," mused Mr. Falcucci. "It's very tempting to act on a tip which seems to be given with the best of intentions. After all, I'd kick myself if I didn't buy a stock I'd been told to buy which then proceeded to treble in price."

"I know the feeling," I replied. "This is what I think you should do. When you are recommended to buy a stock, first check whether the market as a whole is rising or falling. In other words, are you in a bull market or a bear market? If the latter, stay out. The odds are against you.

"If the market as a whole is strong, check how the stock you have been recommended is behaving. Is it rising or falling? Has it been behaving strongly recently? Is it near its high or low for the year? If the stock is acting strongly I would buy it. If the stock does not seem to be doing very much, leave it alone until there is a breakout, then buy it on the breakout. In both cases when buying protect yourself with a stop-loss of, say, 10 percent. This is absolutely essential but nearly always overlooked. In addition, never be temped to hold on to your stock once it has started to fall. Never give back more than 20 percent of your profit.

"None of these precautions require any extensive research or knowledge. You can quickly find out what you need to know by just looking in the newspapers. But never buy a stock blindly just on somebody's say-so. By taking these simple precautions, together with the first-class tips you are getting from these rich Americans, you'll soon be in a position to buy up the hotel!"

Mr. Falcucci guffawed and Mr. Klein laughed. We all got up and stretched. I suddenly felt very tired and realized to my surprise that the hotel lounge was completely deserted except for the three of us. I glanced at my watch. It was two in the morning! No wonder I felt dead beat—we had been talking for over five hours. It had been an illuminating, instructive, and sobering evening. Not only had Mr. Falcucci and Mr. Klein had their eyes opened, but I had learned a lot from their questions too. Their portfolios, their queries, and their feelings reminded me very much of my own early groping days in the market. I had made my own fair share of mistakes, but I had learned from my errors and turned them to my advantage.

"Well, I hope I have been of help," I said. "There's only one other thing to say."

"What's that?" they asked.

"Here's to your first million," I said jokingly, raising my glass.

I could still hear them laughing as I wearily made my way to bed.

MR. FALCUCCI'S PORTFOLIO

Disney	IBM
Digital Equipment	Eastman Kodak
Eastern Gas and Fuel	Amcord
Howard Johnson	General Motors
McDonald's	Equifax
Grolier	Merrill Lynch
AT & T	Basic, Inc.
Pittston	Reynolds Metals
Polaroid	American Broadcasting
Boeing	AMBAC
MCA	Automation Industries

MR. KLEIN'S PORTFOLIO

Avon	Loew's
Champion Homes	Data General
Levitz Furniture	Skyline

Xerox
Joy Manufacturing
Ponderosa
Schlumberger
Tandy
TelePrompTer
ITT
National Semiconductor
3M

Ashland Oil
American General Insurance
Automatic Data
Babcock and Wilcox
General American Oil
Sante Fe International
Bangor Punta

MR. DARVAS' PORTFOLIO

Teledyne
Mitchell Energy

Houston Oil
Bally

Dar·Card©

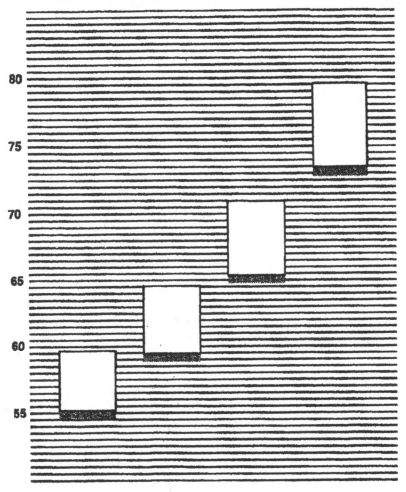

PART III
How to Build Your Own Portfolio

My late-night talk with my old and good friends, Mr. Falcucci and Mr. Klein, about their stock investments did not end the matter as I had fully expected. The reason it did not was that I became fascinated with these two portfolios. Not in the usual sense to be sure—there was nothing especially surprising among their holdings, or at least no stocks or situations with which I was not already familiar. No, the fascination came from quite another aspect of these portfolios.

The next morning, when I found them both neatly typed on the night table where I had placed them before retiring, it struck me that each was a little museum of stocks that had attracted attention in the late 1960s and into the 1970s. These had been trying years for many investors—the events of these years had caused me to rethink my own ways of operating and return to the strict implementation of my own tried-and-true trading rules. With Mr. Falcucci's and Mr. Klein's portfolios in hand I could return in time and attempt to discover the past anticipations that had led to these recommendations.

After all, this had been Mr. Falcucci's and Mr. Klein's investing method—buy the stocks their distinguished guests recommended.

The Hotel George V is the crossroads for the sophisticated and informed of the world; and, by pinpointing the reasons given at the time for buying the stocks in these two portfolios, I would have a very good cross-sectional view of the hopes and fears that were motivating investors in these years when the whole world seemed to be changing directions and heading into uncharted waters.

What had these unsettling years done to the ways that knowledgeable international investors looked at stocks?

Had they been re-examining their assumptions and methods even as I had during these years?

If so, was there any evidence that they had learned new techniques that could help me in my own investing?

Naturally, I was very excited by the time I reached the lobby that morning. I could hardly wait to see Mr. Falcucci and Mr. Klein and begin my search for any signs that international investors had become more knowing and realistic in their stock selection methods in the troubled market climate that we had been experiencing since the late 1960s.

But my hopes were quickly dashed by Mr. Falcucci. When I explained why I needed to know the names of those guests who had recommended each of his stocks in the past, he merely smiled, shrugged his shoulders, and said:

"Oh, I understand very well what you want and why you want it. But I am afraid I can be of little help. You see, I am a busy man, and I couldn't for the life of me remember who first told me about the stocks in my portfolio."

Mr. Klein was equally unable to recall who first called his attention to the stocks he had in his portfolio.

This left me with a frustrating morning. I had an exciting idea—chronicling the changing investment philosophies of knowledgeable international investors—but I had no way to put it into operation. Finally, it occurred to me that there was a way to get this plan into motion even if Mr. Falcucci and Mr. Klein had forgotten their original informants. Each week at the Hotel George V there is a considerable turnover—people coming and going to all of the farflung corners of the globe. For many it is like returning home; so conversation is free and easy. All I would need to do is turn the conversation toward stocks—particularly the stocks of the last ten years.

It has been my experience that, while some people are reluctant to talk about their current stock holdings, almost everyone is quite willing to talk and reminisce about the stocks they once owned. Not that some of this reminiscing may not be colored, or recalled a bit inaccurately through the mists of the past; but for the purposes of my survey even slightly distorted pictures will serve— I was not interested in whether they actually made money in the stock (let alone how much), only in why they *thought* they were going to make money in the stock. A company actually reporting deficits can have rising stock prices if enough people *anticipate* that it will be operating in the black tomorrow.

So I went to lunch quite happy. With only a few weeks of "research" in the lobby, the lounge, and the bar of the Hotel George V, I could come up with the reasons why people thought they could have made money in stocks like the ones in the portfolios of Mr. Falcucci and Mr. Klein.

At lunch Mr. Falcucci supplied me with an unexpected bonus. He came over to my table and told me that he did recall one recommender. The stock was Grolier and the tip had come from Max, the manager of another of Paris's well-known hotels. The reason he recalls this recommendation is that it was an early one, among the first stocks he ever bought; so this one stood out in his mind.

That very afternoon I was able to get started. Max paid the George V one of his periodic courtesy calls. And I was able to ask him:

"Mr. Falcucci and I were discussing his stocks the other night. He remembers buying Grolier and to the best of his recollection you were the first to tell him of this stock. Do you remember making such a recommendation?"

"It has been a long time, but yes, I remember why I bought Grolier and why I told Mr. Falcucci to buy. It can all be summed up in one word: Sputnik."

"Sputnik?" I replied, somewhat amazed. "But what does the Russian satellite have to do with a encyclopedia company?"

"Oh, it is all quite simple. You see, in my hotel we have conventions and international conferences. One time they discuss energy. Another time they discuss ecology. This time there was a meeting of publishers from all over the world. The Russians had just launched Sputnik and were the first into space, and there was much talk of the United States catching up. This meant education, and I reasoned that students learn out of books; so I asked around the publishers' convention. I was looking for a company that published books that every American family would want to buy their children. If everybody has to get smarter to catch the Russians, then no family will want their children to lag behind; so they will buy them books. And so we come to Grolier."

"You make it all sound quite plausible. But tell me, do you still own Grolier?"

"No. I sold it years ago."

"And did you tell Mr. Falcucci to sell? He may well be left holding a stock that reached a high of 38 and has had trouble getting above 3 in the last couple of years."

"In all likelihood I did not. In fact, I seldom tell anyone to sell. If they do not own the stock, then I am
merely boring them with my sell advice. And if they own
a stock I am selling, then I run the risk of alienating
them; so I only say positive things about stocks to my
friends and acquaintances. As the host of a major international hotel I cannot afford to give my guests any
reasons for sleepless nights."

"That is understandable," was all that I felt I could
muster in the way of a reply, making a mental note to
myself that possibly the only thing worse than an
amateur investor is an amateur investment advisor.

At this point Max offered the following suggestion:
"If I understand correctly what you are attempting,
then there is a permanent guest in my hotel you should
meet—the Countess Albanese. Her title is genuine
enough, her late husband, the Count, having all the right
pedigrees. She herself was once an American show girl,
and I believe she was Miss Iowa in a year that her best
friends do their best to forget. She has an extensive stock
portfolio. And her husband, being considerably older
than she, took great pains to teach his wife to be a
widow; so she will know the whys and wherefores of
every stock in her portfolio."

I was delighted with Max's offer, and a few telephone
calls later I was having dinner with the Countess Albanese in the well-appointed main salon of her hotel that
evening. She proved to be quite charming and, although

an American by birth, her long residence in Europe had turned her into one of those capable continental women with competence in almost all of the departments of life, knowing not only where the best cuts of meat are to be found in a city but where the price is right as well.

Over dessert I launched my inquiry: "Max tells me that you are a skilled and knowledgeable investor."

"Max is a flatterer. Whatever wisdom I may have acquired in this area I inherited from my husband, along with the stocks in my portfolio."

"And what kind of stocks did your husband accumulate for you?'

"I am deep in the conventional 'widows and orphans' stocks. The Count was always wary of brokers, feeling that some unscrupulous market operators tend to prey on unsuspecting widows by churning their accounts for the fees involved; so he put me into stocks that appeared safe to buy and hold. For instance, I own a large block of AT & T. How conventional and safe can you be?"

"I couldn't agree more with the Count about the shabby ways of brokers, but I would like to know a little more about his 'buy-and-hold' philosophy. Why did he feel that AT & T was necessarily safe for the long haul?"

"Basically, the Count relied on the fact that AT & T has nearly three million stockholders. This gives AT & T a potent political lobby; and, with its rates subject to regulation by the government, the telephone company has need of political clout. Any threat to the earnings of

AT & T might cause at least some of its three million investors to write letters to their congressmen. This is why I have not worried about the recent antitrust actions against AT & T. Whatever the outcome, it is unlikely that the government will let three million small stockholders suffer permanent and irreversible damage.

"And, of course, there are few things that a company can sell that are more attractive than a means that permits us all to talk more over greater distances."

"You may be right," I said, in as noncommital and diplomatic a manner as I could, "but why bother with the stock? AT & T may be 'safe' enough, but it goes nowhere. Why not get as good a return with fewer worries in Telephone bonds?"

"While I am comfortable, I need to dip into my principal every now and then when I need a little luxury. Still, in all I try to be practical. If I held bonds, I would have to take relatively big bites out of my holdings, close to a thousand dollars at a time. This would tempt me to be extravagant. No, I am happy with my stocks. I can tailor the sales more to my needs; and, if I plan ahead, I am often able to sell my stock at a very favorable time and earn a little something extra, something I would almost never be able to do with bonds."

"I applaud you. You seem to have done what very few investors have managed—find an investment plan that they understand and that suits their needs. Of course, your plan would not do for me; I like action. And you have more courage than I when it comes to the market. When a stock stands still, year in and year out, like AT & T, I am always afraid that it is going to lose its balance and plunge down almost out of sight."

I looked at Mr. Falcucci's list. "How about IBM? Was that a stock to buy and hold?"

"But of course. IBM is another stock I never worry about. My husband was always impressed with the fact that more investors' dollars were tied up in the common stock of IBM—some $35 billion when the stock trades at 250—than any other stock in the world. Again, IBM has had its brushes with the government—it is not in a regulated industry, but when you are as big and dominate your markets like IBM, you have to count on a little envy spilling over on you. IBM is the one to beat; so when you can't beat them in the market, you may try beating them in the courts.

"It is no surprise to me that none of this had diminished the allure of IBM for investors. Money attracts money, and IBM has attracted more investment money than anyone over the years."

"And do you own any more blue chips? How about GM?"

"Oh, yes. But my husband always said that this was something of a problem stock. The company makes motors of all kinds—motors that go in automobiles, refrigerators, locomotives, airplanes. I suppose that is why they call it *General* Motors. But selling motors can be a tricky business. People tend to bunch their buying, and this causes sales to drop every three or four years. So the Count made up this divinely simple rule for me: Consider buying GM any time it drops below 40; consider selling whenever it goes above 80. And it has worked like a charm for me."

"Obviously, you were lucky in love and this has made you lucky in the stock market" appeared to be the only gallant thing to say at this point. We discussed a number of other old-line companies that rank with the bluest of the stock-market chips, but none of them appeared on Mr. Falcucci's list. Having made a date with the Countess to go to the opera, I thanked her for her kind cooperation in my research efforts and said my adieus.

As I was leaving the hotel, I decided to drop into the bar for a nightcap. As I was ordering my drink a young man whom I recognized as having sat at the next table in the dining room addressed me as follows:

"Pardon me, but are you into stocks? I didn't mean to eavesdrop, but I did hear you discussing stocks with the lady."

"You are forgiven; and, yes, you might say that I am 'into' stocks."

At this point we exchanged introductions. By name, he recognized me as a dancer. And I should have recognized him since his face was on posters all over Paris that week. He was a famous rock star in town for a concert. When he found out that I was writing a book about stocks, he made me promise to leave him entirely anonymous. He was afraid that it might hurt him with his fans if they knew that he was interested in such "heavy" things as stocks. So I will call him Mr. Rock Starr.

"Tell me Mr. Starr, what interests you in stocks? For I, like your fans, would never take you for a serious investor."

"Rock acts aren't exactly like Guy Lombardo, you know. I will consider myself lucky if I have a gig to welcome in 1980; so I have to put something on the shelf for when the glitter goes."

"As an entertainer, especially one who must depend on his legs, I know exactly what you mean. But, tell me, what do you have in your cookie jar way up there on the shelf?"

"All I know is entertainment; so I stay pretty close to home. I buy only those companies I know something about. That's why I bought Disney, because that's where I got my start. I was in one of those alternating bands in Tomorrowland at Disneyland. My agent says I shouldn't tell people this—I could get to be known as the Mouse-keteer of Rock. But I was impressed with how clean they kept the place. Anyone that could take one of the sleaziest acts in the business—an amusement park, a carny—and turn it into a Rocky Mountain high deserves an awful lot of credit.

"Not to mention their original act, all of those goofy

cartoon characters. In a town where animal acts are a dime a dozen and there is a Snow White on every street corner, it takes a lot of brains and moxie to even think of drawing make-believe ones. It's a wonder all of the live actors didn't chase them right out of Hollywood.

"But what really clinched it for me was when Old Man Walt died and they kept their act together. That's real style."

"So you are a Disney fan. What else do you have tucked away?"

"I like MCA. They are all over the lot—movies, TV, records. They even run the tourist services at Yosemite National Park. And if you are into reading, they bought a publishing house recently. Every year it gets harder and harder to take some time off from work and not spend some of your old fun dollars with MCA.

"Some people say they were just lucky with their movie *Jaws*, but I don't think so. I think this outfit has plenty of smarts; they did it once; and they know how to do it again. That's why I am going to let my money ride with this one."

"Are there any other spectaculars you own in the world of entertainment?"

"Yes, I have always liked American Broadcasting. Avis was number two and look how hard they tried. Well, ABC is number three, and I think they are trying even harder. There's the TV network; it's been winning a lot of nights away from NBC and CBS. And their local TV stations are in a lot of the biggies—NYC, LA, Frisco, Motown, Chicago. They are in records, publishing; they can even show you scenic and wildlife attractions.

"And there may be a little hidden goodie way down in the bottom of the stocking. They own a Colonial restoration named Smithville near Atlantic City. I know because I played the Steel Pier once. Now that the old roulette wheels are set to spin down by the Jersey shore, who knows? After all, what are the kiddies going to do while daddy is trying to make his point? ABC looks like a company that is in a lot of the right places right now.

"That's all she wrote. Right now, that's my little nest egg. See me next year. If I have moved up the charts, there may be more."

After all of these glitter stocks, I decided it was time to split; so I left Mr. Rock Starr sipping his wine and hailed a taxi to hurry me home to a well-deserved rest after a very full day of stock research.

The next few days were uneventful, until I saw a likely candidate for an interview at breakfast one morning. He was wearing a string tie, a pearl gray suit, and I thought I saw cowboy boots under the immaculate white tablecloth. Of course, he was not wearing a hat, but I had little doubt that his Stetson was somewhere in the hotel. I invited him to breakfast with me. He seemed pleased to accept.

"Name's Tom Burns. I'm from Texas."

"I would have never guessed," I lied. I introduced myself and moved straight to the point, my quest for the investment methods that had been putting stocks in portfolios over the last five or ten years.

"A few years back I could have helped you move your bale of cotton. I used to wrestle with a whole passel of them stocks; but I found out the hard way why they call them rattlesnakes 'brokers'! I went broke under all of that loving care my broker was giving me. He brokered me real good. Now I only own one stock."

"It must be a very fine stock for you to continue to hold it. May I know its name?" I asked, my interest piqued.

"Merrill Lynch," was his reply.

I must have looked dumbfounded because he did not wait for me to ask the obvious.

"I know what you must be thinking. But, you see, I'm only trying to make that cotton-picking company give me back the money they hornswoggled out of me. When the Thundering Herd took me to the cleaners, I hardly had enough money left to get my britches pressed. But I sniffed me out some oil and pretty soon I had me a grubstake. When Marilee Lynch goes down, I buy her; when she goes up, I sell her; and if she pays a cash dividend while I am holding her, I salt that away."

At this point he fished into his suit coat pocket and came up with a leather-bound memo book. He licked his index finger and leafed through the book until he hit the right page.

"See right here. She has already given me back $23,177.10; and the way I reckon it, she still owes me $71,433.15. And she's going to give it all back, even if I have to chase her all over hell's half acre. Meantime, all of the money she has already given me back is waiting for me nice and safe in the Midland, Texas, bank."

I had always heard that it takes all kinds to make a stock market, but I had never really appreciated it fully until Mr. Tom Burns told me how he was trading in Merrill Lynch for revenge.

That afternoon I came across my old friend John McMahon in the lobby reading the Paris *Herald-Tribune*. I was surprised because I thought I recalled that his daughter was getting married that afternoon.

"Shouldn't you be upstairs at the wedding reception?"

"Not really. I have already given away the bride, and I loathe her friends; so I am just waiting here until they are all through guzzling it down and I can pick up the tab."

"By the way, haven't I seen you around the hotel quite a bit in the last few years? Don't you own a business in Des Moines? How can you spend so much time away from the shop?"

"I sold the business four years ago. I have a new line now. You might call it buying into the business cycle."

"But isn't that dangerous?"

"It could be. But I only buy into the upturn phase of the cycle. I buy them in the gloom and I sell them just after the first bloom has begun to fade. This way, while everybody is getting the jitters and asking each other what's going wrong, I am off chasing the sun."

My antennae went up. I remembered a number of cyclical stocks in Mr. Falcucci's portfolio. "Were you here in Paris in early 1975?"

"Yes, I was. In late 1974, the gloom had become so thick in the United States that you could cut it with a knife; so I knew it was time for me to buy in. I placed my orders and escaped to Paris for a little emotional release from the gloom and doom at home."

"Did you tell Mr. Falcucci about your purchases?"

"You mean to tell me that he bought them? Well, no harm done. I still own them myself. My three favorites then were a cement maker, a maker of refractories for steel mills, and a basic metal producer, as depressed and gloomy a lot as you will ever find near the bottom of a business downturn.

"My cement choice was Amcord. It has a lot of the features I like to see in a stock. For one thing, it recently changed its name from American Cement. Some investors think they have made a brand-new discovery, and some of those who may have been burned in it before may be lured back again. And it has relatively few shares, some of them closely held. This adds a scarcity feature and helps keep the pot boiling when things start to move. Its plants are spread right across the map—some in the Far West, others in the Midwest, and a few on the East Coast. Amcord also does part of its business in metal buildings, many of them with industrial applications, warehouses, and the like. This only heightens the cyclical nature of their business.

"Basic Inc. was my choice in steel. The company's chief business is granular products used largely to maintain steel-industry furnace linings—and not many of those furnaces are getting new linings at the trough of a business cycle. If that is not enough downside potential for you, the company also makes electronic devices used in a number of heavy industrial machines. Want to go lower? The company rounds out its product line with a group of industrial chemicals, some of them used in such recession-vulnerable lines as building products, rubber, pulp, and paper.

"There is also a trading bonus in the form of a very thin issue. There are less than 1.3 million shares of common stock outstanding, some of them closely held. So once this one starts to move, it is pretty hard to catch.

"Reynolds Metals rounds out my recession trio. The second largest U.S. aluminum producer, Reynolds takes its lumps when industry uses less metal. Not as much as the other two. After all, it has managed to pay some cash dividends each year since 1941. And there are more shares available for public trading than I like to see, some sixteen million outside the Reynolds family holdings. But it's my quality entry, my hedge stock in case I moved prematurely."

Mr. McMahon had just finished his masterful presentation of the cyclical approach to stock-market trading when he was paged, and he and his checkbook were asked to rejoin the wedding party. I would have liked to have asked him more about his approach since, in a way, it is quite different from mine. While I am very sympathetic to the idea of buying at the right time in the business cycle, I feel more comfortable when my stocks tell me that a recession is coming (or a recovery is underway), rather than the other way around. Some cycle bottoms are unmistakable, but there are those that leave you wondering: how low is low?

High technology, certainly one of the leading stock categories of the late 1960s and early 1970s on the market, had failed to surface under my present research methods even though there were several such situations on Mr. Falcucci's list. This called for a special strategy, and the best one I could think of was a visit to Rene Dupré, an international scientist of great repute who still had both feet planted firmly on the ground and could sort out the science from the fiction, both in the laboratory and on the stock market. I had submitted my list of stocks in advance; so Mr. Dupré was ready and waiting for me when I arrived:

"I am not surprised that none of your investors mentioned the high-technology stocks. Few people have any idea what they are buying when they buy high technology—all of the companies seem to be busily perfecting 'little black boxes,' with one box looking much like the other on the surface. Even scientists working in a field have difficulty telling, in advance, which little black box will work.

"Realistically, about the only thing that an investor interested in high technology can tell in advance with any degree of certainty is whether he is getting his high technology undiluted or mixed. That is, whether he is investing into a one-concept, one-product company, or whether he is buying a mix of sciences and technologies. Also whether the technology is linked to government or the private sector.

"Take Boeing on your list. Its mix splits pretty well right down the middle—half military, half commercial airline. What happens is, to a large degree, beyond the control of the company. If you are trying to time your purchase here, you will want to know all you can about future defense needs and the equipment needs of the world's airlines. Those who bought in here in the early 1970s apparently thought both these needs were in gear and headed up.

"Automation Industries is another company on your list that splits down the middle—half government, chiefly navy, and half something else. It is in the 'something else' that the chief difference comes between Automation

Industries and Boeing. Unlike Boeing, Automation provides a wide variety of specialized industrial products, technical services, and materials-testing equipment to a wide spectrum of industries. Not all of these lines are equally profitable and, paradoxically, that is one of the chief attractions Automation has had for investors over the last few years. The company is busy weeding out and selling off its less profitable lines, hoping to emerge at the other end as a stronger, more consistently profitable operation.

"If it is diversification you are seeking, AMBAC Industries will answer nicely. It is virtually a consortium of formerly independent, strongly science-oriented divisions—American Bosch, Packard Instrument, Bacharach Instrument, Arma, to name just a few. And it has capabilities in a number of exciting new fields: medical instruments, diesel fuel injection (it is building a prototype of a Ford-designed gasoline fuel-injection engine), electrical equipment. It's in both the government side and the private sector of the high-technology advance.

"If you want to specialize and concentrate your fire in high technology, then Digital Equipment makes a good vehicle. It does over 80 percent of its business in minicomputers. These miraculous little computers already perform a wide variety of highly specialized tasks in recording, interpreting, and doing computations on data emerging from scientific experiments. They have been adapted to processing business data. And each new series brings new applications and uses. But there is a catch. This exciting new frontier in computers is also the most highly cyclical, the most intensely competitive area in the general computer field. Right now Digital is the top dog, but tomorrow the winner is likely to be the firm with the stop sales force.

"What it comes down to is that if I want to hedge my bets in high technology, I would go with a company like AMBAC. On the other hand, if I wanted to take some extra risks in pursuit of better-than-average gains, I might try a company like Digital."

"Or, in other words, you are telling me that in high technology it makes more sense to watch the market than to puzzle over the potentials in all those little black boxes?"

"Precisely. Now you have also asked me to tell you what I think attracted investors to a number of applied technology fields, energy and the like. I think I can be helpful here.

"Pittston, being a holding company, puts you into a number of energy-related fields. One of its subsidiaries mines and sells high-grade metallurgical coal, chiefly to the steel industry, which adds a cyclical spin to earnings results. Another big chunk of their business is in the wholesale distribution of petroleum, predominantly heating oil in the New York City area. Branching out from its oil distribution is an extensive trucking and warehousing operation, also in the New York area. It also owns 85 percent of Brink's, the armored-car service. All in all, a steady and dependable citizen in the energy field, its chief stock-market appeal being its cyclical run-ups in periods of business recoveries. It would be my guess that this is what put Pittston on your list in recent years.

"Eastern Gas & Fuel is another solid citizen in the energy field. Boston-based, it has widely diversified interests in energy. Its coal subsidiary is the ninth largest producer in the U.S., with mines in West Virginia and Pennsylvania and western reserves estimated at 2.5 billion tons. Boston Gas, a wholly owned subsidiary, serves almost five hundred thousand customers in eastern Massachusetts, including the Boston area. In addition, Eastern Gas is the largest tonnage carrier on inland waterways in the U.S., operating on the Ohio, Illinois, Arkansas, and Mississippi rivers. With all the recent concern about energy sources, both in the U.S. and around the world, it is hardly surprising to find it in a portfolio assembled over the last decade.

"Now Equifax takes us into another area of applied technology. Formerly Retail Credit, the company is a leader in insurance investigation and credit reporting. Faced with the problem of assembling, sorting, and retrieving literally millions of bits of information, the company is atttempting to bring in cost efficiencies through computerization. It was these cost-control programs that helped reverse the downtrend in earnings and undoubtedly was a factor in putting Equifax on your list. Healthy growth in its insurance investigation and credit rating work also probably helped."

I complimented Mr. Dupré on the breadth of his knowledge and his pithy expression of the essentials in each of the situations I had given him for review.

When I returned to the hotel, I found a message waiting for me. The name—a Mr. Charles Raymond—was unfamiliar, but I decided to return the call.

The voice on the other end of the line sounded hesitant. "As a rule, I do not volunteer. I learned that a long time ago in the army. But my grapevine tells me that you are looking for the tipsters responsible for Mr. Falcucci's portfolio. I think I can be of some help. He has probably forgotten, but I was in and out of the hotel quite a bit just after his mother's estate was settled; so naturally enough we had many conversations about financial matters, including stocks."

Needless to say, I was delighted. We met in the lobby. Mr. Raymond proved to be a jolly, hearty man, with independent means. Although born to wealth, he appeared most understanding and willing to be of help to those of us who had neglected to include sizable inheritances among our natural endowments.

"As I was riding over in the taxi," Mr. Raymond started as soon as he was seated, "I thought back on those days. I had an investment philosophy then. Perhaps it can best be summed up in the old GE slogan: Better things for better living. The United States had already become affluent, and the rest of the world was itching to get there. So I always asked myself how the products made by a company whose stock interested me could bettter things for people, make them more comfortable.

"In the U.S. some of this affluence was paid for by women entering the work force. Some of these women may have gone back to work for the traditional reason, to keep the wolf away from the door. But I do not think this was true for the majority of newly working women. They were there to provide the little extras, the luxuries that were difficult to afford on their husbands' wages alone. That is why I always like the fast-food companies, McDonald's in particular.

"McDonald's always had the right idea. Keep it simple; keep it cheap. This way the working wife can take the family out without feeling guilty. She can indulge herself and still have some change left over to provide some luxuries. And it must be working. I understand they are adding over four hundred units a year, not only in the United States but all around the world. Why, they are even here in Paris!

"For the same reasons, I have always been interested in Howard Johnson. Travel has always been a popular luxury, all the way back to the last century when the well-to-do used to take Grand Tours of Europe. And today is no different. But when you travel with children, as so many Americans do today, you want no surprises.

And Howard Johnson has done the best job in providing a familiar, comfortable environment for the traveling family.

"And when they travel, they take pictures, which brings us to Eastman Kodak, another of my long-term favorites. It's the world's largest producer of photographic products, and it got that way by providing reliable, easy-to-use products, all the way from the Brownie to the Instamatic camera.

"But let's not forget Polaroid. Its on-the-spot developing process has revolutionized the industry. There were two giant breakthroughs that put Polaroid where it is today: First, black and white and then color. And there may be more where those came from.

"Now, of course, Eastman and Polaroid are slugging it out in the marketplace, each with its own version of the instant picture. I know that everyone is thinking of this battle of the titans in the field as a win-or-lose situation, but I take a different view. Isn't it possible that they both may win, to the benefit of the consuming public, and the investing public as well?

"Well, these were my humble suggestions for Mr. Falcucci's consideration. I have no idea whether he acted on them; but, if he did, I am confident that he will live to celebrate them."

"I hope you are right, Mr. Raymond. I hope you are right," was all I could say after this amazing display of unshakable investor confidence. As Mr. Raymond retreated through the lobby, I could not shake the conviction that I had just been visited by the Ghost of All Bull Markets Past.

Although Mr. Raymond's recital had been unrewarding in some respects, it had finally brought me to the end of my self-assigned task. I had stirred up old memories, old expectations and anticipations. And, now I had some pretty solid reasons why the stocks in Mr. Falcucci's portfolio had been recommended to him by his guests.

And what had I learned?

First and foremost, I had learned that, despite the sharpest market shake-out since the 1930s, the current breed of investors had not changed their spots. Tidbits of information here, a slight trace of sense over there, a twice-told and often misunderstood story at yet another time was chiefly what they relied on to put their hard-earned money to work in the stock market.

Second, I had learned yet again that there is no real substitute for a comprehensive plan when it comes to investing. This plan must be capable of taking you in and getting you out, as well as protecting you all those perilous days when your money is riding in the troubled waters of the stock market.

My experience with Mr. Falcucci's portfolio left me with little heart to tackle Mr. Klein's. I was convinced that, while I might meet a lot of charming people in the process of conducting my investigations, in the end I would be no wiser. My time would be spent more profitably in reviewing the techniques that had stood me well over the years.

So I decided, instead, to review my own current portfolio. It had but four stocks: Teledyne, Mitchell Energy, Houston Oil, and Bally.

Appendix

I am often asked to give a brief, simple summary of my method and principles—what one might call the Darvas System in a nutshell. The basic principles of my method are in fact quite simple.

Firstly, except in exceptional circumstances I only buy the stock of companies in new and developing industries, i.e., companies whose growth and earnings prospects look highly promising. I never buy stocks in established industries, in companies with huge capitalizations, or in companies which are already so big that the prospect of any further substantial growth is highly unlikely.

This does not mean that I only buy stocks of companies making useful or promising products. If some new craze is born I will not hesitate to jump on the bandwagon if an opportunity presents itself, no matter how absurd or bizarre the craze may seem. If a yo-yo or hula-hoop craze sweeps the world, the stocks of the yo-yo and hula-hoop manufacturers will soar. It would be silly not to take advantage of such fads, whatever one might think of yo-yos and hula hoops.

Secondly, having found such lively stocks I certainly do not buy them straightaway. I first check the overall market trend to ascertain whether stocks in general are in an uptrend. I then check whether the stock belongs to a strong industry group, i.e., a group that is performing well in the market relative to other groups. Only when I have satisfied myself on these two points do I look in more detail at the stock that interests me.

Why all these precautions? Because I like to be sure that the odds are in my favor. If the market is in a downtrend and the industry group is performing weakly I know that the cards are stacked against me and that my chances of making big profits are poorer than if the market and the industry are strong. You cannot be too careful in the stock market.

Of course there are exceptions to the rules. There have been any number of stocks that have multiplied in price manyfold in a bear market, just as there are plenty of stocks that have hardly moved in a bull market. But my temperament is such that I prefer to be safe than sorry. So I keep out in a bear market and leave such exceptional stocks to those who don't mind risking their money against the market trend.

Having decided that the investment climate is right and that the industry is right I am ready to buy the particular stock if it is rising in price on high volume. My basic principle of stock-market investment is that the only valid reason for buying a stock is that it is rising in price. If the price is rising no other reason is needed; if the price is not rising no other reasons are worth considering. I am not the slightest bit interested in explanations of why it is behaving as it is, and I am even less interested in explanations of why it is *not* behaving as it was expected to. I am only concerned with realities, in what is actually happening, not in conjectures, alibis, projections, rationalizations, and excuses.

I would then study the behavior of the stock in the light of my "Box Theory." My early studies and observations of stock price movements had revealed to me that the price movements of active stocks were not, as had at first appeared, a series of erratic and random price changes but a series of price ranges or boxes. Thus a stock over a period of days or weeks might vary and close anywhere between, say, 30 and 38—never going below 30 and never moving higher than 38, i.e., its movements would be confined within a narrow "box," the top of which was 38 and the bottom 30.

Then, suddenly, one day, for no apparent reason, the stock would forcefully break out of its box either on the upside or downside and move into another box, which might either overlap the previous one or be entirely separate from it. Thus a stock originally varying randomly in a 30–38 box might suddenly jump to a 40–46 box or decline to a 25–32 box, within which it would again fluctuate randomly.

I found that the entire upward (or downward) progress of stocks consisted of a series of movements of this kind—a progression from one box to another. Each stage in the progress of a stock was marked by a period of random variations between well-defined box limits, followed by a breakthrough, then a further period of random variations between new box limits, and so on. The price movement of a stock, in short, appeared to take place in a series of jumps from one box to another. The day-to-day random fluctuations that occurred inside each box were irrelevant—they simply marked a stage in the onward march of the stock. All that was really needed to size up the situation were the boxes within which the prices moved.

Once a DAR-CARD of the boxes has been drawn, the problem of when to buy is solved immediately. *The right moment to buy a stock is when it is in its topmost box and it breaks through the top of this box into new high ground.*

Thus if a stock is in a 30–35 box, say, and this was its topmost box, I would place an order with my broker to buy it as soon as it reaches 35¼. No further considerations were needed.

Since I first started using this automatic buying method over twenty years ago stock markets have changed. In recent years I have found that a penetration above the top of the box is often immediately followed by heavy selling which drops the stock a couple of points and drives it back into its previous box again. A purchase on a first penetration can therefore lead to a considerable loss. The reason for this behavior may be that astute professionals and floor traders know that a penetration above a resistance level is a signal for chartists to rush in and buy, so the professional traders take this opportunity to unload stock and thus make a point or two. In view of this I now wait for a second penetration before buying, i.e., a penetration above the top of the topmost box, a downward reaction, and then a further rise to a *new* high above the first penetration's high. It is well worth taking this extra precaution. If the price does not drop back after the first penetration but goes on rising I leave the stock alone; I never chase a rising stock because I never know when it will turn round and drop back again.

What if no suitable stock satisfying these criteria is available? I just sit on the sidelines and wait for one to come along. I have often remained liquid for as long as two years if I could find no stocks worth buying. I never buy a stock unless it seems likely to at least double in price in six to twelve months. If no such stocks come to my attention I prefer to be out of the market altogether. Why should I put my money at risk in the stock market with the chance of losing 50 percent for the sake of a paltry 10 percent return when I can get much the same return with *no* risk by simply keeping it in Eurodollar bonds?

Many people seem to think they must always keep

their money "working," i.e. constantly invested in stocks. They just hate to go into cash. But why remain invested in a bear market when everything is dropping? Why ride the market up and down and lose on the downside what you have so painstakingly made on the upside?

There are even some people who believe that a policy of "buy and hold" is the best, so they hang on through thick and thin. Presumably they get some masochistic pleasure from seeing their capital melt before their eyes every two or three years in successive bear cycles, or they just close their eyes, grit their teeth, and sit it out. With that sort of approach stock-market investment becomes a succession of nightmares. I prefer to sleep soundly at night, even if it means going into cash for long periods.

When do I sell? This for most people is the most difficult problem of all and yet it is on the answer to this question that success or failure really depends. You may have picked a perfect stock and bought it at exactly the right time but if you hang on too long or sell too soon you may either end up with nothing or miss an enormous profit.

As long as a stock remains in its topmost box or is in a clear uptrend I am perfectly content to stay with it. But I know that sooner or later the trend is going to reverse and the boxes are going to come tumbling down. So I prepare myself for this before it happens. *I give my broker advance instructions to sell my stock if the price falls through the bottom of its topmost box.* The reason for this is as follows. If a stock is in a 35–40 box, say, it can bounce up and down between these limits as often and as long as it likes. I don't care how often it hits 35. But if it falls through the bottom of the box it is obvious that something significant has happened to weaken its support and there is therefore no knowing how far it will fall before establishing itself in a new lower box. The bottom of the box is thus the obvious point to sell out. As a stock moves up I, of course, reset my stop-loss to the bottom of the next higher box and so on.

I look on the stop-loss as a sort of safety net which I fix under me to prevent me falling too far and suffering serious financial loss if my stocks nose-dive. And such it has proved to be. Time and again it has saved me from disaster when the market and my stocks turned round and went into a decline. I never enter the market without it.

Some years ago a well-known author wrote a book on investment in which he devoted a whole chapter to denouncing what he called "the evils of the stop-loss." The use of the stop-loss, he claimed, leads straight to bankruptcy. You would never get the impression from reading the chapter that stocks ever went down or that there were such things as bear markets. In the wonderful stock-market world described by many writers on the subject stock prices only go up, the market always behaves rationally and logically, money is as easy to make as falling off a log, and there is no need to protect yourself against mistakes or market downturns. Unfortunately the stock market they describe bears little relation to reality, as anyone who enters the market with such a rose-tinted view will soon discover to his cost. Many people who were all but wiped out in the 1969–70 and 1973–74 bear markets would have given their right arm to have had the foresight to use a stop-loss. For them it was the lack of a stop-loss, not the use of one, that led straight to bankruptcy.

Sure there are times when I sell too soon or get stopped out on a false move, but I have never been caught in a bear market and that makes up for any number of minor errors. Even today, after twenty years in the stock market, I still treat stocks with the same respect a lion tamer has for his lions—although he is the master he is well aware that they can give him a nasty injury if he is foolish enough to be reckless and lower his guard. So, in the same way, when I enter the stock-market jungle I make sure that my quick escape route, the stop-loss, is close at hand.

When I bought Teledyne and Mitchell Energy and Development in 1976 I used exactly the same method I have just described—a combination of market observation, my Box Theory as illustrated visually on the DAR-CARD, and my protective stop-loss. I had first noticed Teledyne in the summer of 1975 when I was scanning the highs and lows. I noticed that it had risen from 9½ to a high of 25¼. This enormous percentage rise in such a short time attracted my attention so I decided to check on it further. I found that the company was engaged in avionics, specialty metal alloys, semiconductors, etc.— just the sorts of things that had always been on top of my list of advanced products of the future. I decided to keep the stock under observation and make a pilot buy if it showed signs of going higher.

But like the market in general nothing much happened—the stock continued to trade sideways right until the end of 1975, never going above 25¼. In January 1976, however, Teledyne suddenly jumped to 27. I immediately placed a buy order and heard later from my broker that he had purchased the stock at 27½. I quickly put in a 10 percent stop-loss to protect myself against the possibility that the move was a false breakout. However, Teledyne didn't drop back. On the contrary it soared higher and higher, with barely a reaction. There was not a single box between 27 and 53! Eventually, in March, Teledyne formed a 47–53 box, giving me a chance to decide my next move. I decided I would buy more stock if it went above 53.

But once again the unexpected happened. Teledyne dropped below the bottom of its box and I was sold out at 47. It fell to 41 and then almost as quickly turned round, rose rapidly and formed a new 55–62 box. I made up my mind to buy it again if it rose above 62. I told my broker to buy it back for me at 62½, which he did within a few days. In the middle of June Teledyne once more took off and within a month was firmly established in a new 67–80 box, where it still is at the time of writing.

My decision to buy Mitchell was influenced by much the same factors—it was a so-called energy stock similar to Houston Oil, it strongly resisted the downward market trend, and it rose strongly on high volume in late 1976. It was obviously attracting considerable attention. I bought it after a stock split at 31⅛ and watched it rise steadily to over 41 in less than a month. Now it is still in a 35–41 box. If it rises further I shall have made a tidy profit; if it collapses I shall be sold out around 35. One thing is sure: I will not merely sit and wait—I will neither lose sleep nor bite my nails nor call my brokers. My method and stop-loss will do all the work for me until the time that Houston, Mitchell, Bally and I part company.

A falling stock's Dar·Card°

Dar·Card°

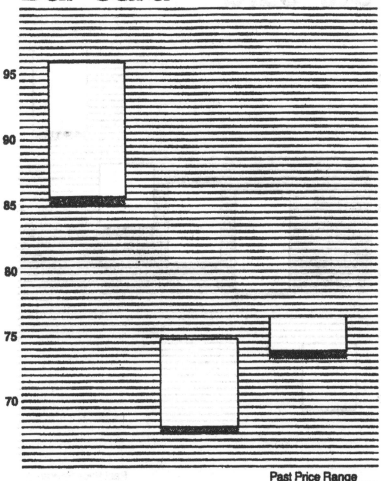

Past Price Range		
1974	97	75
1975	81	65
1976	76	65
	High	Low

A rising stock's Dar•Card°

Dar•Card°

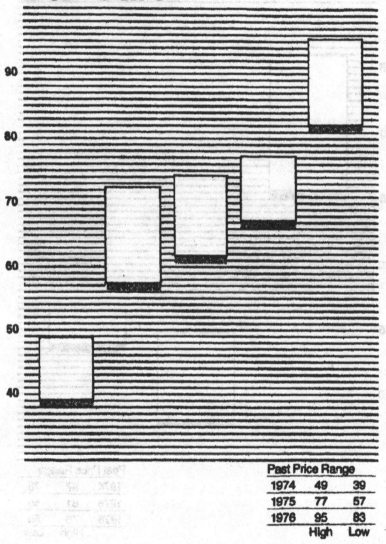

Past Price Range		
1974	49	39
1975	77	57
1976	95	83
	High	Low

Dar·Card° as short-sale indicator

Dar·Card°

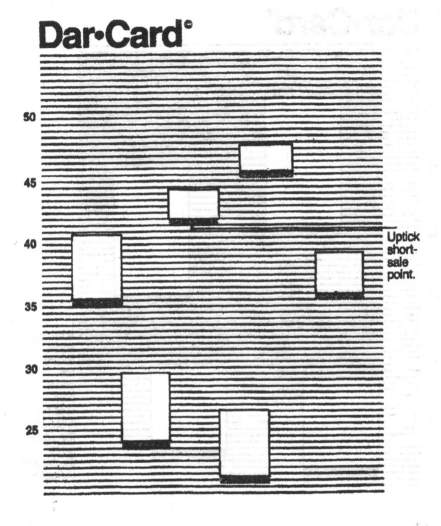

Uptick
short-
sale
point.

Dar·Card©

95

90

85

80

75

70

A falling
stock
ready
for
short
sale
(selling
rules are
the same
as in
the buying
indicator).

138

A rising stock's Dar·Card°

Dar·Card©

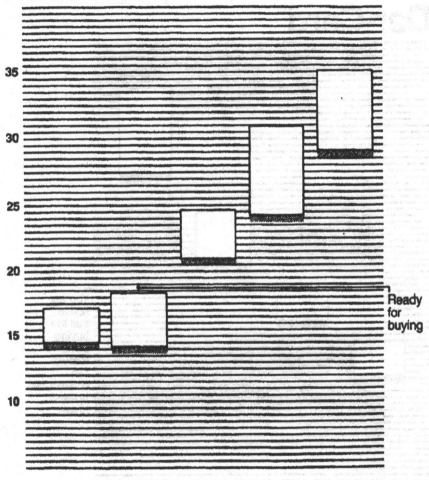

Ready
for
buying

139

A Helping stock's Dar-Card.
Dar-Card

Dar·Card°, buying indicator

Dar·Card°

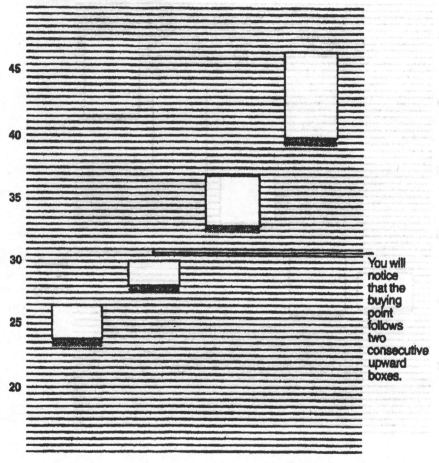

You will notice that the buying point follows two consecutive upward boxes.

Dar•Card©

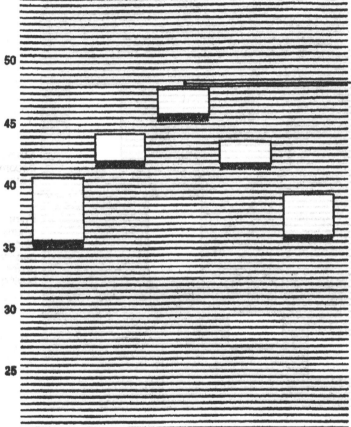

"Must buy and order immediate stop sale in the first shaded area following the buy.

147

Dar•Card°

Stock becomes a buy.

Point where stock is gearing up for buying.

TEST YOURSELF!

How will these outstanding 1976 performers behave in 1977? Up? Down?

A & J INDUSTRIES

ADDRESSOGRAPH

AHMANS

AMBAC

AMCORD

AMERICAN
  BROADCASTING

AMGNIST

ASHLAND OIL

AUTMIND

AUTOMATIC DATA

BOEING

CENTRONIC DATA

DATA GENERAL

DIGITAL
  EQUIPMENT

GENERAL MOTORS

McDERMOTT

McDONALD'S

SANTA FE
  INTERNATIONAL

SUNDSTRAND CORP.

TEST YOURSELF

these will show outstanding rapid performance reduce
in 1979, U.P. Dowes.

A & J INDUSTRIES	BOEING
ADDRESSOGRAPH	CENTRONIC DATA
ALLMANS	DATA GENERAL
AMBAC	DIGITAL
AMCORD	EQUIPMENT
AMERICAN	GENERAL MOTORS
BROADCASTING	McDERMOTT
AMCRIST	McDONALD'S
ASHLAND OIL	SANTA FE
AU TMIND	INTERNATIONAL
AUTOMATIC DATA	SPERRY RAND CORP.

Recommended Readings

•Technical Analysis of Stock Trends, Robert D. Edwards, John Magee, www.bnpublishing.net

•Wall Street: The Other Las Vegas, Nicolas Darvas, www.bnpublishing.net

•The Anatomy of Success, Nicolas Darvas, www.bnpublishing.net

• The Dale Carnegie Course on Effective Speaking, Personality Development, and the Art of How to Win Friends & Influence People, Dale Carnegie, www.bnpublishing.net

• The Law of Success In Sixteen Lessons by Napoleon Hill (Complete, Unabridged), Napoleon Hill, www.bnpublishing.net

• It Works, R. H. Jarrett, www.bnpublishing.net

•Darvas System for Over the Counter Profits, Nicolas Darvas, www.bnpublishing.net

• The Art of Public Speaking (Audio CD), Dale Carnegie, wwww.bnpublishing.net

• The Success System That Never Fails (Audio CD), W. Clement Stone, www.bnpublishing.net

CPSIA information can be obtained
at www.ICGtesting.com
Printed in the USA
LVHW031035220623
750492LV00006B/14